DYLAN THOMAS
A JOURNEY FROM DARKNESS TO LIGHT

DYLAN THOMAS

A Journey from Darkness to Light

by

Alphonsus M. Reddington, O.F.M. Conv.

PAULIST PRESS

New York, N.Y.   Glen Rock, N.J.

Amsterdam   Toronto   London

ACKNOWLEDGMENTS

Dylan Thomas, COLLECTED POEMS. Copyright 1939, 1942, 1946 and © 1957 by New Directions Publishing Corporation. Copyright 1937, 1945 by the Trustees of the Copyrights of Dylan Thomas. Copyright 1953 by Dylan Thomas. Reprinted by permission of New Directions Publishing Corporation.

Dylan Thomas, QUITE EARLY ONE MORNING. Copyright 1954 by New Directions Publishing Corporation. Reprinted by permission of New Directions Publishing Corporation.

Dylan Thomas, ADVENTURES IN THE SKIN TRADE. Copyright 1939, © 1964 by New Directions Publishing Corporation. Reprinted by permission of New Directions Publishing Corporation.

Dylan Thomas, LETTERS TO VERNON WATKINS. © 1957 by New Directions Publishing Corporation. Reprinted by permission of New Directions Publishing Corporation.

Library of Congress
Catalog Card Number: 68-31049

Published by Paulist Press
Editorial Office: 304 W. 58th St., N.Y., N.Y. 10019
Business Office: Glen Rock, New Jersey 07452

Printed and bound in the
United States of America

Contents

PART I
THE NATURE AND METHOD
OF THE JOURNEY

PART II
THE JOURNEY IN ITSELF

PART I

The Nature and Method
of the Journey

I

INTRODUCTION TO THE
THREEFOLD NATURE
OF THE JOURNEY

"Dark is a way and light is a place"

In 1934, Dylan Thomas answered a question from the editor of *New Verse* by describing his poetry as "the record of my individual struggle from darkness towards some measure of light." [1] This statement is crucial because it is the key to the central preoccupation of all of Thomas' poetry: a personal effort to give meaning to himself and the world by exploring certain basic philosophical, moral and theological problems. This dominating quest gives coherence and consistency to the entire body of his poetry.

Paying tribute to Thomas at his death, George Barker, a fellow poet, alluded to this unity and consistency of his achievement:

The poems as they are make up a complete and working body, a natural organism, a shape and pattern fulfilled and functioning, like a fly's eye or a stellar pattern, so that retrospectively, one could believe that he had not died too soon. [2]

A growing awareness of this organic structure of Thomas' poetry has led critics, as G. S. Fraser observed, to seek a formula which would explain it. [3]

[1] Dylan Thomas, *Quite Early One Morning* (New York: New Directions, 1954), p. 188.
[2] George Barker in *Dylan Thomas: The Legend and the Poet—A Collection of Biographical and Critical Essays*, ed. E. W. Tedlock. (London: Reinmann, 1961), p. 72. (Future reference to this volume will be to Tedlock.)
[3] G. S. Fraser, "Dylan Thomas," *A Casebook on Dylan Thomas*, ed. John

3

David Aivaz, one of his best critics, expounded the view that "process . . . is the basic theme of all Thomas' poems." [4] He explains process as "unity in nature; its direction is the cyclical return; the force that drives it is the generative energy in natural things." [5] There can be no doubt that such an explanation can serve as a useful guide to much in both Thomas' method and meaning: to his method—because the energy like the heart of a Thomas poem is both constructive and destructive:

> The force that through the green fuse drives the flower
> Drives my green age; that blasts the roots of trees
> Is my destroyer. [6]

to his meaning—because it accounts for the oneness of his world. Life and death are no longer two states but the same course of energy. Likewise, the absolute is no longer distinct from the creation but is present in the flux. This notion would explain the pantheism of much of Thomas' early poetry.

But would the concept of "process" offer Thomas a satisfactory answer to the kind of questions he was asking? Not unless the poet was willing to accept life as a giant squirrel cage, a meaningless round of days in which the individual life has no significance. Aivaz himself admits that "process" is not the whole story; he maintains that "the problem of reconciliation—of the individual with the general process—is a major theme in Thomas' poems." [7]

One solution to this problem, as Aivaz sees it, is that Thomas did more than entertain a philosophy of process; he actually undertook to "celebrate" the process. [8] This view is shared by other critics, notably David Daiches. [9] But one might again question,

---

Malcolm Brinnin. (Further reference to this volume will be to *A Casebook*.) (New York: Thomas Y. Crowell Co., 1960), p. 47.

[4] Tedlock, p. 195.

[5] *Ibid*.

[6] Dylan Thomas, *The Collected Poems of Dylan Thomas* (New York: New Directions, 1957), p. 10. All page numbers in parentheses following quoted poems are to this volume.

[7] Tedlock, p. 202.

[8] *Ibid*., pp. 202-206.

[9] David Daiches, "The Poetry of Dylan Thomas," *College English*, XVI (Jan., 1954), pp. 50-61.

would not the celebration of the process, in itself, be likewise meaningless, unless the process had become meaningful to man?

Daiches is aware of this difficulty and tries to reconcile it by observing that Thomas did not arrive easily at the notion of celebration, but "moved to it through disillusion and experiment" [10] to understanding. Only in his later work, Thomas realized that death, the destroyer, could not destroy him. Death could only release him for immortality in eternal life. At this point he had "progressed . . . to a period of more limpid, open-worked poetry in which, instead of endeavoring to leap outside time into a pantheistic cosmos beyond its dimensions, he accepts time and change, and uses memory as an elegiac device." [11]

Aivaz, one concludes, agrees with Daiches. This is a logical inference from the statement towards the end of his essay, that "process . . . needs man to 'happen' to it to give it life. . . . In Thomas' later poems especially, vision seems not only to celebrate process, but also to inform it." [12] Moreover, Aivaz assures us that there is no contradiction between the idea of the cyclical return of the process and the "linear" movement in Thomas' journey from darkness to light: "It requires only that the mind and heart evolve an ever fuller relationship to it." [13]

Perhaps a truer evaluation of Thomas' poetry is achieved if it is examined not merely in reference to the "process," not merely in reference to its "celebration," but in reference to Thomas' ever-evolving "vision" of it. This view goes more profoundly to the roots of the journey which Thomas proposed to be taking by focusing upon his internal conflicts—the subject, as we shall see, of all his poetry. As they are worked out in his poems, these conflicts either detain or advance him on his journey toward an understanding of self, others, and the world. The term, "vision" (often used in Thomas' poems, and later borrowed as a critical label by Aivaz), [14] as used in this book refers to the gradual

[10] *Ibid.*, p. 53.
[11] *Ibid.*, p. 57.
[12] Tedlock, p. 206.
[13] *Ibid.*, p. 210.
[14] *Ibid.*, p. 200.

unfolding of Thomas' philosophical, moral and theological understanding of his basic conflicts.

These internal conflicts are reflected in a series of dualisms
throughout Thomas' poetry. The most basic of these antitheses is
that of light and darkness, which Thomas himself mentioned.
Flowing from these two are a host of others. The following are the
most representative: life (resurrection) and death; eternity (immortality) and time (mortality); creation and destruction; certi-
tude and doubt; soul and body; innocence and sin; love and sex;
union and isolation; trust and fear; joy and grief; peace and suffering. For clarity and convenience, the sources of conflict will be
reduced to three major heads, relating to philosophical, moral
and theological issues, respectively. This plan occasions a consideration of Thomas' journey (which will be undertaken in Part II
of this book), from three points of vantage: "From Death to Life
(Chapter III); "From Sin to Innocence" (Chapter IV); "From
Doubt to Faith" (Chapter V). In the remainder of this chapter,
we will be solely concerned with establishing the fact that philosophical, moral and theological issues were the basic concerns of
Thomas' poetry.

Although John Sweeney,[15] in his introduction to the *Selected
Writings of Dylan Thomas,* spends several pages showing the
influence of the metaphysical school poets—particularly, Donne,
Marvell, Vaughan, and Herbert—still it should be made clear
that the term "metaphysical" as used in this book is given not its
usual literary significance but its philosophical sense. It refers,
therefore, to the science of being or the first causes of all things.
This metaphysical proclivity at the heart of his poetry is implicitly
contained in the following statement by Thomas:

A good poem is a contribution to reality. The world is never the
same once a good poem has been added to it. A good poem helps
to change the shape and significance of the universe, helps to
extend everyone's knowledge of himself and the world around
him.[16]

[15] John Sweeney (ed.), *Selected Writings of Dylan Thomas* (New York:
New Directions, 1946), pp. xvi-xxi.
[16] Thomas, *Quite Early. . .* , pp. 192-193.

If one should overlook this fundamental metaphysical attitude in Thomas' poetry, one misses the whole point of his poetry. Then one is tempted to raise the specious objection, voiced by John Wain [17] that Thomas' poetry is too narrow in subject matter. Indeed, Geoffrey Grigson, in an essay more perverse than perceptive, accuses Thomas of having not a theme but an obsession with birth, death, and love, expressed in an unstructured array of images.[18]

This type of criticism was definitively demolished by two distinguished critics, Elder Olson [19] and David Aivaz; [20] neither of these men applies the term "metaphysical" to Thomas, but both demonstrate that he was a dialectically complex poet, a poet who thought before he wrote and who had something significant to say. Thomas himself would have been the first to contend that he wanted to be heard for his sense even more than for his sound. In fact, he admonished his close friend and fellow poet, Vernon Watkins, for suggesting changes in his poetry that might improve it aurally, but which overlooked the integrity and value of what he was trying to say.[21] It can be said without punning that Thomas was deadly serious about the special kind of knowledge that his poetry offers.[22] Few critics have grasped Thomas' intention with greater perspicacity than D. H. Savage:

Thomas is a poet to whom the overworked epithet "metaphysical" may without unfitness be applied. He is a poet preoccupied not primarily with human experience as it is commonly apprehended, but with aspects of experience lifted out of their apparent context and seen in extra-mundane relationship to their absolute, vertical, determining conditions. Central to his work, therefore, is a proto-philosophical, impassioned questioning of the ultimates—origins

[17] "Dylan Thomas, A Review of His Collected Poems," *A Casebook*, p. 69.

[18] *Ibid.*, p. 119.

[19] Elder Olson, *The Poetry of Dylan Thomas* (Chicago: University of Chicago Press, Phoenix Books, 1961), pp. 36-39.

[20] Tedlock, p. 210.

[21] *Dylan Thomas: Letters to Vernon Watkins*, ed. Vernon Watkins (New York: New Directions, 1957), p. 66.

[22] Harvey Breit, in "Talks with Dylan Thomas," *A Casebook*, p. 197, quotes Thomas as saying, "I like to think of it [poetry] as statements made on the way to the grave."

and ends—of existence. . . . His theme is thus that of the human condition itself, . . . the essential or fundamental "existential" human state, . . . the condition of being, itself.[23]

Critics who overlook Thomas' fundamental philosophical concern, frequently overlook, in addition, his fundamental moral concern. John Sweeney has punctured the meaningless objection that Thomas' poetry lacks social consciousness. Sweeney points out that Thomas was concerned primarily with the regeneration of the individual; his contemporaries (Auden, Day Lewis, Mac-Neice, Spender) were more interested in the regeneration of society.[24] Thomas' attitude was novel when it appeared. But a change in value and attitude came with disillusion and war, and "the individual self is now the compositional key." [25]

Noting this strong, personal element in Thomas' work, William York Tindall commented that "no matter what the ostensible subject of his prose or verse, Thomas always wrote about himself." [26] Francis Scarfe echoes this judgment by describing Thomas' poetry as "entirely autobiographical." [27] If it is autobiographical, it is not so in the ordinary sense of the word; that is, a true record of persons and external events which influenced or shaped the writer. Rather, it is a spiritual autobiography because it records the internal conflicts—emotional, psychological, intellectual, moral and spiritual—that the soul encounters in its journey through the darkness of the *Inferno* towards the light of the *Paradiso*. In this journey, Thomas descended a long, long way down to the first frontiers of his psyche, and he discovered that he was a creature at war with himself. As he phrased it:

I hold a beast, an angel, and a madman in me, and my inquiry is as to their working, and my problem is their subjugation and victory, down-throw and upheaval, and my effort is their self-expression.[28]

[23] "The Poetry of Dylan Thomas" in Tedlock, pp. 141-42.
[24] Sweeney, p. x.
[25] *Ibid.*
[26] William York Tindall, *A Reader's Guide to Dylan Thomas* (New York: The Noonday Press, 1962), p. 16.
[27] "Dylan Thomas: A Pioneer," *A Casebook*, p. 33.
[28] Quoted by Suzanne Roussillat in Tedlock, p. 14.

Despite this impressive statement of intentions, Karl Shapiro contends that Thomas ultimately failed to actualize them. He conceives of Thomas as the perpetual child helplessly tossed between the two poles of joy and despair because he lacked the intellectual stamina necessary to bridge the gap between life and death, self and the world.[29] According to Shapiro, Thomas' poetry reveals "no transition, no growth."[30] All that Thomas achieved, he achieved through some "undefined mystique"[31] since he had no "true philosophical or religious substance to fall back upon."[32]

Shapiro is correct in pointing out that there are conflicts in Thomas' poetry which stem from the contradictory forces in his own nature. These account for the tension in his poetry and help to explain his poetic method. Thomas was not always successful in resolving these tensions, in balancing the contradictory forces in his poems. On such occasions, when his writing fails to come to that "momentary peace which is a poem,"[33] this method seems mere trickery. It hopelessly obscures whatever he is trying to say. Elder Olson masterfully appraises the situation in the following passage.

When the conception underlying his poem is a powerful and lofty one, and controls all the devices of his poem, Thomas is magnificent; when the conception is trivial, or when the treatment of it does not sufficiently manifest it, he is utterly disappointing. His art demands great energy of thought and passion and all the accoutrements of the grand style; when the high conception is wanting, energy becomes violence and noise, the tragic passions become melodramatic or the morbid, ecstasy becomes hysteria, and the high style becomes obscure bombast.[34]

But to say that Thomas sometimes fails, is not the same as to say that he never succeeds. Shapiro's accusation, however, that he

[29] "Dylan Thomas," *A Casebook*, p. 174.
[30] *Ibid.*, p. 177.
[31] *Ibid.*, p. 174.
[32] *Ibid.*, p. 169.
[33] Henry Treece, *Dylan Thomas: "Dog Among the Fairies"* (2nd ed., rev.; London: Ernest Benn Limited, 1956), p. 37.
[34] Olson, *op. cit.*, pp. 23-24.

attained neither transition nor growth implies that Thomas never
succeeded in bringing these contradictory elements into harmony. All the major critics—Aivaz,[35] Moynihan,[36] Olson,[37] Tindall,[38]—give testimony to the contrary. If Shapiro misses this
point, it would seem that he overlooks or dismisses as "undefined
mystique" the dialectical argument that constitutes the heart of
Thomas' method. Admittedly, the dialectic argument is complex.
The various dualisms (previously noted) are not treated in isolation but are mingled together in a single poem. The relationship
between the elements in any of these dichotomies is further com-
plicated by the fact that the argument between them, although
rational, is shot through with emotional and unconscious fac-
tors.[39] Such a method is bound to involve a keen psychological
awareness and a tendency to raise moral issues, even if it does not
always arrive at clearly delineated moral decisions. As Thomas
himself remarks in one of his poems, "Dark is a way and light is a
place" (p. 191). It can be expected, then, that as the poet pain-
fully gropes his way through his dark period, trying out solution
after solution, he will reveal himself confused and indecisive at
times. Obviously, to make such a statement is not equivalent to
saying that Thomas did not make moral decisions. Elder Olson
declares that Thomas is continually making moral decisions in his
poetry, but in his early poetry he leaves the reader doubtful as to
the permanency of these decisions.[40] Nevertheless, Olson insists
that Thomas' most distinguishing characteristic is that he is "a
poet of the internal moral workings of the soul." [41] If the complexity of Thomas' dialectical argument sometimes obscures this
fact, happily, as William T. Moynihan will proceed to demonstrate:

. . . the chronology of Thomas' argument is lyrically simple: the
early work is principally concerned with themes of revolt, the

[35] Tedlock, p. 210.
[36] William T. Moynihan, *The Craft and Art of Dylan Thomas* (New York:
Cornell University Press, 1966), p. 216.
[37] Olson, *op. cit.*, p. 20.
[38] Tindall, p. 184.
[39] Olson, *op. cit.*, p. 37.
[40] Olson, *op. cit.*, p. 40.
[41] *Ibid.*, p. 33.

middle work with themes and situations of reflection and debate, the late work with themes of praise and consent.[42]

This brings us to the last section of this chapter—the theological roots of Dylan Thomas' poetry. Although the critics disagree among themselves in defining the nature of Thomas' religious interest, all of the major critics agree that Thomas was a religious poet. G. S. Fraser, Stuart Holyrod, E. Glyn Lewis, W. S. Mervin, Elder Olson, Kenneth Rexroth, D. S. Savage, Edith Sitwell, John L. Sweeney, William York Tindall, and Amos Wilder, all uphold this position.[43] The last-mentioned critic offers a representative statement:

The work of this poet is . . . most significant as an index of that breakthrough to a deeper level of awareness consequent on the cultural pressures of our time. There is here a continual exploration of man at an existential level which as in the work of all the most significant writers of our time can only be called theological in its implications.[44]

Biblical imagery constitutes an essential fibre of the whole body of Thomas' poetry; indeed, almost every page of the *Collected Poems* contains some biblical reference. As Thomas himself exclaimed:

> I know the legend
> Of Adam and Eve is never for a second
> Silent in my service. . . . (p. 145)

It is not our contention that Thomas was ever wholly orthodox in his Christianity (the use of the word "legend" should make this clear) even at the end, but it is our contention that the religious issue is at the core of his work throughout.

[42] Moynihan, *op. cit.*, p. 159.
[43] Fraser in *A Casebook*, p. 53; Holyrod, *ibid.*, pp. 139-152 Lewis in Tedlock, pp. 172-185; Merven in *A Casebook*, pp. 59-67; Rexroth, *ibid.*, p. 130; Savage in Tedlock, p. 143; Sitwell in *A Casebook*, p. 125; Sweeney, Selected Writings. . . , p. x; Tindall, *A Reader's Guide. . .* , pp. 8-9; Wilder, *Modern Poetry and the Christian Tradition* (New York: Charles Scribner's Sons, 1952), pp. 100-102.
[44] Wilder, *Modern Poetry. . .* , pp. 100-101.

Surely, his Welsh nonconformist background is largely responsible for such religious concerns. Thomas' great-uncle on his father's side of the family was a Unitarian minister; on his mother's side, his grandfather was a deacon, one uncle was a preacher, and another was a minister of a Congregational church. When he was a child, Thomas attended the Castle Street Congregational Church with his mother and sister. He kept on the wall of his room the Sunday School certificate which he won.[45] To say just when Thomas became skeptical of the form of Christianity presented to him or just how much he was influenced in this direction by his father (whom he describes not so much as an atheist or agnostic, but as a man angry with God)[46] is most difficult to establish.

Although Thomas later rebelled against his childhood religion, his poetry clearly proves that he never got religion out of his system. Feeling that religion was needed to give meaning to his world, he resolved this ambivalence by elaborating a personal religion: a blending of Christianity (treated mainly as myth or fable in his early poems) and other forms of belief which he borrowed from Welsh Druidism and the occult.[47] It will be shown that in his journey out of the darkness of confusion and rebellion, he did achieve a measure of light.

We do not mean to imply that one finds a theological system—anymore than a philosophical one—worked out in Thomas' poetry. To understand, however, what he was striving for, one must be aware of the philosophical, moral and religious roots of his poetry. The difficulty is compounded by the fact that Thomas was not using the language of either philosophy or theology. His was the language of poetry, characterized by a very personal idiom. G. S. Fraser sums up the problem in these words:

Though Thomas' attitude to life was, as he grew older, an increasingly religious, and in a broad sense an increasingly Christian one, he was certainly not a poet, like Mr. Eliot, for instance, to

[45] Bill Read, *The Days of Dylan Thomas—A Pictorial Biography* (New York: McGraw-Hill Paperbacks, 1964), pp. 20-24.

[46] *Ibid.*, p. 22.

[47] E. Glyn Lewis, "Dylan Thomas," in Tedlock, p. 173.

whom dry theological and metaphysical speculations were, in themselves, poetically exciting. His world was not a conceptual world and his coherence is not a conceptional coherency.[48]

In the next chapter, we will discuss Thomas' method of creating this non-conceptional world.

[48] *A Casebook*, p. 53.

II
THE METHOD OF THE JOURNEY
"The womb of war"

Conflict creates the fire of affects and emotions, and like every fire it has two aspects: that of burning and that of giving light. Emotion is on the one hand the alchemical fire whose heat brings everything to light and whose intensity . . . burns up all superfluities, but on the other hand emotion is the moment where steel meets rock and a spark is thrown off. Emotion is the chief source of all becoming-conscious. There can be no transforming of darkness into light and of apathy into movement without emotion.[1]

From the beginning the most striking characteristic of Thomas' poetry was its revelation of his awareness of a dynamic universe, where the essential drives of nature within and without man are simultaneously destructive and constructive. This awareness found its most usual expression in a preoccupation with birth and death as physical and spiritual processes, in a constant use of both sexual and religious experience as both subject and symbol, and in an employment of correspondences between the human and non-human spheres of existence. These antitheses are both a key to his handling of theme and image and the inevitable outcome of his poetic method. This method is expertly described in Thomas' own statement, which, though long, deserves quotation in its entirety:

A poem by myself needs a host of images, because its center is a host of images. I make one image—though "make" is not the word. I let, perhaps, an image be "made" emotionally in me and

[1] Jolande Jacobi (comp. and ed.), *Psychological Reflections—An Anthology of the Writings of C. G. Jung* (New York: Harper & Bros., "Harper Torchbook" ed., 1961), p. 32.

then apply to it what intellectual and critical forces I possess—let it breed another, let that image contradict the first, make of the third image bred out of the other two together, a fourth contradictory image, and let them all, within my imposed formal limits, conflict. Each image holds within it the seed of its own destruction, and my dialectical method, as I understand it, is a constant building up and breaking down of the images that come out of the central seed, which is itself destructive and constructive at the same time. . . . The life in any poem of mine cannot move concentrically round a central image, the life must come out of the center; an image must be born and die in another: Out of the inevitable conflict of images—inevitable, because of the creative, recreative, destructive and contradictory nature of the motivating center, the womb of war—I try to make that momentary peace which is a poem.[2]

This passage, over and above the help it affords in locating the genesis of whatever ambiguities and obscurities are contained in the poetry of Dylan Thomas, offers a lead for consideration of three aspects of his use of imagery. Each of these demands attention: the emotional association of images, the rational and critical control of these images, and their antithetical development.

Emotional association of images is one of the chief techniques of modern poetry. C. Day Lewis observes that from the Symbolist movement through the many succeeding movements that helped to create modern poetry, emphasis has been laid upon the illogical, even the irrational, in opposition to the classical emphasis upon the cause and effect sequence of images. Lewis' explanation is that the modern poet is writing about a complex and unsettling time; that he is trying to rescue the almost atrophied imagination of a public whose analytic faculty and taste for information is overdeveloped; and, finally, that the modern poet is trying to break through the web of self-consciousness, which seems the peculiar burden of modern man, as well as through a skepticism which refuses to be impressed by the poet's craft.[3]

Whatever the practical reasons might be, Jacques Maritain has

[2] Quoted by Treece, *op. cit.*, p. 37.
[3] C. Day Lewis, *The Poetic Image* (New York: Oxford University Press, 1948), p. 122.

provided the esthetic explanation and justification of modern poetic practice.[4] According to Maritain, the modern poet differs from the classical poet in trying to preserve throughout his poem the creative intuition—the internal music or intuitive pulsion—which initially sparked the poem. The modern poet, therefore, asserts the primacy of the "poetic sense" over the "logical sense" because the logical sense is only one of the components of the "poetic sense" and, as such, "is entirely subordinate to the poetic sense, through which the poem exists."[5]

Stephen Spender, in a review of the *Collected Poems of Dylan Thomas*, recognized this practice in Thomas and succinctly described it in the following passage:

A powerful emotion—we may suppose—suggests to Dylan Thomas an image or a succession of images, and it is these which he puts down, without bringing forward into consciousness the ideas which are associated with such images. He suppresses the intellectual links between a chain of images because they are not sensuous.[6]

To maintain that Thomas' images originate in and are developed by emotional impulse is not to say that the process itself is not subject to rational and critical control. The popularly-accepted view—that there is a total absence of such control—can be proved false by an examination of Thomas' manuscripts, as is pointed out by Louis MacNeice, himself a convert from the popular view.[7]

Another misconception of Thomas' work rates it as surrealistic. This position cannot be seriously defended by anyone who accepts the definition of Surrealism given by its founders.

Pure psychic automatism, by which it is intended to express . . .

[4] Jacques Maritain, *Creative Intuition in Art and Poetry* (first reprint ed.; New York: Meridan Books, 1955), Chaps. VII and VIII.

[5] *Ibid.*, p. 192.

[6] Stephen Spender, "A Romantic in Revolt," *Spectator*, CLXXXIX (Dec. 5, 1952), p. 781.

[7] Louis MacNeice, "The Strange, Mighty Impact of Dylan Thomas' Poetry," *The New York Times Book Review*, April 5, 1953, p. 1.

the real process of thought. Thought's dictation, in the absence of all control exercised by the reason and outside all aesthetic or moral preoccupation.[8]

Thomas himself refers specifically, as has been noted, to the formal limits which he imposes upon his image making, and to the rational and critical control which he applies to them. Moreover, many competent critics have attested to the truth of his statement and confirmed it by a rigorous analysis of the "argument" in his poems.[9]

If any comparison is made between the work of Thomas and the Surrealists, it must be based only on a superficial similarity in the use of words. Modern critics have distinguished two qualities in a word: its utility as a thing, and its utility as a referent or an indicator. Various terms have been formulated to distinguish these two qualities: affective and logical; emotive and cognitive; opaque and transparent, and the like. The Surrealists tried to telescope these two qualities of words, somehow hoping that the sole use of the word as a thing could do the whole work of poetry.[10]

Like the Surrealists, Thomas is very "thing" conscious; but unlike them, he supports his sound with sense. As J. Bayley has pointed out, Thomas' poetry "often means and sounds physically: the sensation is that we are being assaulted by some means other than words." [11] Wanting to assault his readers with reality and knowing that the poet's best way to accomplish this is through an appeal to the readers' emotions, Thomas kept his poetry as sensuous as possible by avoiding direct statement and by suppressing the logical connections between his series of images. But to say that Thomas thus freed his poetry from the primacy of the logical organization of ideas, is not to say that in it there are no ideas

[8] Quoted by Geoffrey Bullough, *The Trend of Modern Poetry* (London: Burns and Oates, 1948), p. 214. The founders of Surrealism were Andre Breton and Philippe Soupault who put forth their doctrine in *The Magnetic Fields*, written in 1921.

[9] See above, p. 7.

[10] J. Bayley, *Romantic Survival—A Study in Poetic Evolution* (London: Constable, 1957), pp. 188-89.

[11] *Ibid.*, p. 215.

expressed. As J. Maritain explains, in treating poems that are obscure in essence because of the technique spoken of above:

Concepts and conceptual utterances may take up a great deal of room, but, because they are then submitted to the mental regime of imagination, not of logical connections, and to the nocturnal law [the obscurity of feeling] which presides over the stirring of images, they hardly convey any explicit intelligible sense.[12]

By means of his towering imagination, Dylan Thomas attempted to close the gap between language and reality. To make immediate and actual what simile or metaphor would leave distant or merely possible, Thomas employed symbols, in the use of which, according to Lawrence Durrell, he was uncommonly gifted beyond any of his contemporaries.[13] Thomas employs not only the usual natural and conventional symbols, but he makes abundant use also of private symbols.

An example of one of Thomas' frequently used private symbols is that of the "tailor," which is repeatedly used throughout "Once below a time" (pp. 147-49), and alluded to directly or indirectly in many other poems. It can be used as a creation symbol: God is described as "the cloud perched tailors' master with nerves for cotton" (p. 148), it can be used as a symbol for human makers, the poets, and is so used derisively of some of Thomas' contemporaries:

> I astounded the sitting tailors,
> . . . . . .
> The flashing needle rock squatters,
> The criers of Shabby and Shorten,
> The famous stitch droppers. (p. 147)

"Tailor" can also be used to describe the fitting of the suit of the flesh, birth symbol; or, since birth is the first step toward death, a death symbol of the poet crouched in tailor fashion in the womb, sewing a shroud for a sail to navigate the sea of life. (p. 110)

[12] Maritain, p. 196.

[13] Lawrence Durrell, *Key to Modern British Poetry* (London: Peter Nevill, Ltd., 1952), p. 197.

Thomas uses many other private symbols, the meaning of which might not be discovered in the words taken singly, but which becomes clear in comparative contexts, for example, "wax" used for dead or mortal flesh; "oil" for life-force; "plum" for the male seed.[14]

Whatever difficulties the reader encounters with Thomas' symbols, metaphors, or images, whatever initial bewilderment over his language techniques, cannot be traced to Thomas' willful courting of obscurity. He said that he liked to think that his later poetry was clearer and deeper than his early work.[15] In order to strip himself of darkness, he felt the obligation to enter into darkness. He tried to bring into consciousness that which previously was blurred by feeling or rested vague and fuzzy in the unconscious. At the same time, he wanted to retain a sense of the groping and struggle that went into the discovery. When Thomas succeeded, he was magnificent. The satisfaction that his reader attains at such moments can best be expressed in J. Bayley's words:

Although by its very nature poetic language is bound to turn feeling into thought, . . . when the process takes place in poetry we retain the mysteriousness and the joyfully hidden quality which existed before the transformation; the sense of thoughts that lie too deep for words, even though—by some miracle—we are reading these words on the printed page.[16]

When Thomas failed, it was because he "was not successful in making a momentary peace with my images at the correct moment," [17] as he tells us.

The effort of rational control was always there, even in his antithetical development of images. If, however, one demands of Thomas' formal discipline a concentric development of all the images from some central image, one shall be disappointed. The reason is simple. As Thomas said in the quotation that heads this

[14] Olson supplies a glossary (pp. 97-101) for these and many other obscure and private symbols of Thomas.
[15] Thomas, Quite Early. . . , p. 166.
[16] Bayley, pp. 196-97.
[17] Treece, p. 37.

chapter, his poems do not develop out of a central image, but out of a host of images, "the womb of war."

In just what way do the various images contradict each other? As C. Day Lewis observes, Thomas apparently is not speaking of logical contradictions, nor of those seventeenth-century conceits in which there is a kind of physical antagonism between image and idea, nor is he speaking of mere verbal free association. What Thomas seems to mean is the bringing together of objects that have no natural affinity; or, perhaps more accurately of objects which would not, on the face of it, seem to make for consistency of impression.[18]

The root of this use of antithesis lies in Thomas' metaphysical explanation of the universe as "process," so evident in his early poems.[19] The following excerpt from one of these poems can be used to illustrate this:

> A process in the weather of the heart
> Turns damp to dry; the golden shot
> Storms in the freezing tomb.
> A weather in the quarter of the veins
> Turns night to day; blood in their suns
> Lights up the living worm.
>
> A process in the eye forewarns
> The bones of blindness; and the womb
> Drives in a death as life leaks out. (pp. 6-7)

In these warring images, the reader is presented, of course, with the obvious contraries: damp versus dry; golden or burning versus freezing; night versus day. But there are, in addition, such seeming incompatibles of the imagination as these: weathers, of the heart and veins; blood, a vital substance, in something inanimate, the sun; bone invested with a consciousness that is able to receive warnings from the eye. Closer examination, however, reveals the method behind the madness. Not only do the images quarrel, but they support and create a quarrel among ideas. The images, then, are not just used as "thing," but as "referents" to the

18 Day Lewis, p. 123.
19 See above, pp. 4-5.

basic argument that death is a part of life.[20] Barely worded in this abstract manner the statement seems trivial and leaves the reader cold, but dressed by the imagination, the words stir the emotions and compel belief. An explication of the imaginative presentation of the theme of these two stanzas reveals the sound, if unique, referential base.

By a practice frequent in Thomas, an analogy is made between the natural world and human nature. The word "weather" does the coupling here, allowing the poet to view the interior of the body as having a climate similar to the external climate of the world. The "process" is not explained, but it carries the suggestion of some organic law to which man is subject as well as nature. It is this idea which is the foundation for the imaginative leap that the poet makes in his comparison. From their context in other poems, "damp" and "dry" may be rightly understood as symbols of life and death, respectively.[21] Consequently, "the weather of the heart" is most likely a mood, which changes thoughts of life towards thoughts of death. Life begins to be transformed into death again at the very moment that the living seed ("the golden shot") is released; for in the cyclical turn of the "process" all things are one; things are born to die, and die to be born again. According to this line of reasoning, the womb may be rightly called the tomb. Even while life is becoming death, death is becoming life: an idea echoed in the second stanza, "the womb drives in a death as life leaks out" (p. 6). And so the interior darkness of the body is lit up by the suns in the blood of the wormlike veins, described as if they contained a fluorescent liquid. But the idea of death predominates and reminds the eye, even as it sees, of the ultimate darkness ("blindness").

This analysis should illustrate that a close, vigorous reading of Thomas is necessary, and that a failure to understand his dialectical method will inhibit one's reading Thomas correctly, if at all. But such an analysis gives an incomplete knowledge of Thomas' complexity. His poems are complex not only because of their "argument," but also because of three lines of activity often present in his poems, which take place almost simultaneously.

[20] Tindall, p. 35.
[21] Ibid.

As stated earlier, Thomas' real inquiry in all of his poetry concerned the workings of the Beast, Angel, and Madman which he discovered in conflict at the very center of his psyche.[22] These three terms might be considered as symbols for desire, reason, and poetic intuition, respectively. This use seems reflected in the following lines of "Should Lanterns Shine," where pulse stands for the energy of the blood or desire, head stands for reason, and heart stands for intuition:

> I have been told to reason by the heart,
> But heart like head, leads helplessly;
> I have been told to reason by the pulse;
> And, when it quickens, alter the action's pace (p. 72)

This interpretation would not be substantially unlike the three-fold conflict of emotion, conscious thought, and unconscious thought, which Elder Olson has pointed out in Thomas' poetry.[23]

Thomas' problem was the ultimate subjugation of these three warring elements either by bringing them to a harmony or by suppressing one or the other of these intractible forces. Nevertheless, his method was not to repress them, but to expose them for better understanding by letting them momentarily live out their contradictory lives within him. Although his object was "to get things straight," [24] he got them straight, indeed, only by first carefully examining their crookedness.

The resulting many-sided conflict in a typical Thomas poem can be illustrated by an analysis of a stanza from "If I Were Tickled by the Rub of Love."

> This world is half the devil's and my own,
> Daft with the drug that's smoking in a girl
> And curling round the bud that forks her eye.
> An old man's shank one-marrowed with my bone,
> And all the herrings smelling in the sea,
> I sit and watch the worm beneath my nail
> Wearing the quick away. (p. 14)

---

[22] See above, p. 8.
[23] Olson, p. 37.
[24] Treece, p. 37.

The title of the poem is surely an allusion to Hamlet's "Aye, there's the rub" in his famous "To be, or not to be" soliloquy. But the speaker in this poem, like Hamlet, is also in a terrible inner turmoil because he desires to do something, but has doubts about its morality and fears its consequences. For stanza after stanza, this poem is built upon a series of suppositions. "If" things were different, the poet would fear neither the reminder of sin and temptation ("the apple"), nor the punishment (the flood; "the gallows," "the axe"); nor his sexual desires ("the devil in the loin"); nor time or death ("the outspoken grave"), to mention only a few. But things are not different, and the speaker can find nothing to assuage him of these fears; so he remains half free and half slave ("The world is half the devil's and my own"). He loves a girl; because the speaker shows no awareness of her as a person but only as an object, it would be more exact to say that he lusts for a girl, any girl. Sex works on him like a drug, so exciting his lust that he is no longer free, but almost out of his senses ("daft"). Still, even as he is attracted, he is repelled. The forked vein of her eye reminds him of the pleasure of the forked loins but also of the punishment of sin, the devil's pitchfork.[25] At the same time, he smells the rottenness of his thoughts like the smell of decaying fish. Torn between fear and desire, like Hamlet, he cannot act ("I sit"). He reflects upon the hasty passage of youth, the old man he is already becoming; and in this mood, he views even the pulse of his blood vessel as a living worm, hastening death by already eating away the flesh.

In the last two stanzas of this poem, after having examined the various kinds of rubs, he decides that the only one that really tickles is "reality." "Rub" stands for some problem or obstacle; at the same time it creates a friction ("the tickle") that is pleasant to the skin or amusing to the mind. The speaker seems to find stimulation, meaning, in the whole mystery of man's condition, which includes his desires, his moral fears, and his fears of old age and death.[26] Thus, having arrived at a decision, the poet concludes with the magnificent last two lines:

[25] Olson, p. 39.

[26] I am indebted to both Olson, pp. 37-39, and Tindall, pp. 46-49 in my interpretation of this poem.

> I would be tickled by the rub that is:
> Man be my metaphor. (p. 15)

Thomas himself is clearly the speaker in the above poem, as he is in several others, for example, "I Dreamed My Genesis," "It Is the Sinners' Dust-tongued Bell," or "I Have Longed to Move Away." There are other poems in which one or more characters other than the poet speak. For instance, "Before I Knocked," "When Once the Twilight Locks No Longer," and "My World Is Pyramid," are "pseudo-dramatic monologues"; "I See the Boys of Summer," "Find Meat on Bones," and "If My Head Hurt a Hair's Foot," are "pseudo-dramatic dialogues." [27] In either case, however, the characters are not true individuals, but merely convenient fronts or masks for Thomas himself.[28] These dramatic devices serve two major purposes: the monologue guarantees imaginative vividness and immediacy of experience that might be lost by third person narration or description; the dialogue projects conflict in action or between diverse points of view or mood.[29] The mask of "the unborn child" in "Before I Knocked" is an example of the former usage, and the masks of "the unborn child" and "the mother" are a case of the latter usage.

Thomas' method of depicting character and activity make it imperative for a reader to remember three important facts. First, whether Thomas himself speaks in his own voice or in that of an assumed person or persons, his intention is single and the same: to make immediate, vivid, and concrete a complex process of activity involving internal moral conflicts which he himself was experiencing. Secondly, Thomas was not content to accept without test what he had been taught was true, especially if that seemed to contradict what he felt, or what he intuitively understood. "Man be my metaphor" (p. 15), he exclaimed, but he was seeking a pragmatical knowledge of man as an existential phenomenon and would not settle for merely theoretical knowledge of man. Thirdly, he was not content to consider life statically; he felt the necessity of viewing life dynamically. Nothing could be clearer than his own statement:

[27] Olson, p. 43.
[28] *Ibid.*
[29] *Ibid.*, p. 44.

I do not want a poem of mine to be, nor can it be, a circular piece of experience placed nearly outside the living stream of time from which it came; a poem of mine is, or should be, a watertight section of the stream that is flowing all ways, all warring images within should be reconciled for that small stop of time.[30]

A poem by Thomas, therefore, could never be as it was for Wordsworth, the result of "emotion recollected in tranquility." Thomas does not offer his readers the calm analysis of a discovery previously made. Rather, he takes his readers with him during the turbulent process of discovery and subjects their minds and emotions to the contradictions which he was immediately experiencing.

In the next three chapters, we will undertake to accompany him through three aspects of his famous journey from darkness to light.

[30] Treece, p. 37.

PART II

The Journey in Itself

III

FROM DEATH TO LIFE

"Death is all metaphors"

Throughout his life Dylan Thomas was haunted by death, who sat like the "old man of the sea" on his shoulders. This preoccupation with death and time (death's agent) dominates the whole body of Thomas' poetry, but it is especially evident in his early work. Commenting on this fact, Karl Shapiro said that he knew of no poet writing in English who used death as a major image more than Thomas.[1] The preponderance and intensity of this concern are frequently attributed to Thomas' early premonition that he was doomed to die young.

Edith Sitwell attested that Thomas had such a presentiment,[2] but the most authoritative testimony was supplied by Thomas' wife, Caitlin, who angrily reported that Thomas believed he would die before forty.[3] She was rankled by her husband's entertaining such a romantic idea and very bitter toward America for offering him the possibility of fulfilling it:

Once again that fiendish element of his days being numbered. . . , and all that sickly, stinking stuff about: It had to be: there was no other way; the illogical, poets must die young, ruthless reasoning that made him follow, nobly and foolishly, that exorable pattern. And it was not necessary at all, not without the baby-snatching seduction: there was no hope, after that; to America.[4]

All men know that they must someday die, but very few are obsessed with the idea as Thomas was. In the light of his poetry,

[1] Karl Shapiro, "Dylan Thomas," *A Casebook*, p. 169.
[2] Edith Sitwell, "Dylan Thomas," *A Casebook*, p. 126.
[3] Caitlin Thomas, from *Leftover Life to Kill*, in *A Casebook*, p. 243.
[4] *Ibid.*, p. 247.

it would seem that what Thomas really feared was not so much the fact of death but the likelihood that there is no life after death. Until Thomas could come to terms with this mystery, life could be no more than MacBeth's "tale told by an idiot, full of sound and fury, signifying nothing" (V, v, 26-28). Thomas attempted through his poetry to pry open the mystery of life and death. Exploding forth hot from the "womb of war," images bumped, multiplied, balanced and contradicted each other. If the structure of his poem could encompass this terrible tension, the poem brought him to "a temporary peace." [5]

Critics generally agree that there are three distinct periods in Thomas' poetry.[6] It is our contention that these periods are not merely distinct, but also represent progressive stages of development.[7] We will, therefore, analyze the death-life conflict (as well as the sin-innocence and doubt-faith conflicts, to be discussed in Chapters IV and V respectively) according to a threefold scheme. In his first period, Thomas presents a sardonic appraisal of his situation which combined a gnawing fear of death with an occasional burst of defiance of it; in his second period, he attempts to shake off his morbid preoccupation with death by giving up his isolation and feeling compassion for other men; in his third period, Thomas reveals not only a joyful celebration of life but also a peaceful resignation to his own impending death.

[5] See above statement on his poetic method, p. 17.

[6] William York Tindall in "Burning and Crested Song," *American Scholar,* XXII (Autumn, 1953), p. 487, says that he and Thomas agreed in a New York bar that Thomas' work fell into three periods and that Thomas accepted the labels which Tindall offered for two of these periods. Tindall called the first "the womb-tomb period" and the third "the period of humanity." Olson (p. 20) describes Thomas' dark middle and later periods. William T. Moynihan, *The Craft and Art of Dylan Thomas* (Ithaca, New York: Cornell University Press, 1966), p. 159, speaks of periods of rebellion, encounter, consent.

[7] Thomas who chose and arranged his poems for *Collected Poems* did not arrange them in their chronological order. See Ralph Maud's "Chronology of Composition" in his first appendix of *Entrances to Dylan Thomas' Poetry* ("Critical Essays in Modern Literature"; Pittsburgh: University of Pittsburgh Press, 1963), pp. 121-148. It is our contention, however, that Thomas arranged his poems in an order which would best reveal the progress of his journey: not progress as he made it chronologically, but progress as he could see it logically looking back.

Elder Olson devoted an entire chapter to describing the universe of Thomas' early poems.[8] In the following sentence he supplies us with a capsule summary of his thoughts on the matter:

It is a nightmare universe of darkness and fright, a world under the "forever falling night" of Time; a world unsaved by Christ, and unsaveable, doomed.[9] (16)

The universe, man, and all other things in the universe were all part of an inevitable and unending "process." Thomas' imagination was excited less by the creative force in the universe, than by the destructive force that made life activity absurd. Thomas' anxiety, guilt and dread in the face of this absurdity have definite affinities with the anguish of the Existentialists. The resemblance is made strikingly apparent in the following passage which describes the philosophy of Camus:

... The absurd man is the lucid man, for he has understood that the world has no meaning; he knows that the universality and inevitability of death made all things to be of only momentary value.

... He is the man of no illusions, the mind of no secret hiding places, for he sees clearly the utter futility of any individual life; he is always conscious of the mad character of human living. Hence the lucid man knows that life is not a matter of explaining and solving but of experiencing and describing.[10]

Although the questions Thomas asked demanded metaphysical answers, his approach was more that of descriptive metaphysics —phenomenological and existential—than that of true ontology. Thomas' primitive or proto-metaphysics of the process developed out of his experience of the world around him. The one certain thing that his experience taught him was that everything in the universe was born to die. He hears the raven speak of death (p.

---

[8] Olson, "The Universe of the Early Poems," *The Poetry of Dylan Thomas* (Phoenix Edition; Chicago: The University of Chicago Press, 1961), pp. 1-18.

[9] Olson, p. 16.

[10] Vincent Martin, O.P., *Existentialism: Soren Kierkegaard, Jean-Paul Sartre, Albert Camus* ("Compact Studies"; Washington, D.C.: The Thomist Press, 1962), pp. 36-37.

19), he sees "the squirrel stumble,/The haring snail go giddily round the flower" (p. 41). Because there is so much evidence of death and so little certainty of life after death, Thomas comes to see himself as

> A cock-on-a-dunghill
> Crowing to Lazarus the morning is vanity
> Dust be your saviour under the conjured soil. (p. 42)

Since the same life force is both constructive and destructive, Thomas found it difficult to conceive of life and death as two distinct states. In the case of human life, the only distinction he seems to allow is that life is a state of consciousness, death one of oblivion. It is difficult to determine more specifically what Thomas thought of the nature of death in his early poetry. Stuart Holroyd believes that it can be compared to the condition of prenatal existence which Thomas vividly described in "Before I Knocked" (pp. 8-9).[11] He detects, at times, a "healthy-minded" attitude toward death in Thomas' poetry, but he concludes that Thomas ultimately reverted to his "pantheistic faith." [12] Derek Stanford understands Thomas to mean that the life of the individual persists after death although not in its natural form:

The life of the individual endures, though with death it changes its mode of existence: the energy of life passes from the body of a person to nourish a wild flower.[13]

If the individual life breaks down into a separate atom of energy which serves the general cosmic purpose, it seems a contradiction for Stanford to say that "the individual endures." He is certainly describing nothing other than the same pantheistic existence mentioned by Holroyd.

There is good reason to believe that Thomas does not believe in any individual immortality in the universe of his early poetry. In

[11] Stuart Holroyd, "Dylan Thomas and the Religion of the Instinctive life," A Casebook, p. 145.

[12] Ibid., p. 146.

[13] Derek Stanford, Dylan Thomas—A Literary Study (First Paperback Edition; New York: The Citadel Press, 1964), p. 76.

"I, in My Intricate Image," Thomas describes the composite nature of man in the phrase "my ghost in metal" (p. 40); "ghost" stands for vital principle, "metal" stands for flesh.[14] In lines reminiscent of Blake's "sick rose," Thomas' creative-destructive force is at work again in this poem:

> Beginning with doom in the bulb, the spring unravels,
> Bright as her spinning-wheels, the colic season
> Worked on a world of petals. . . . (p. 40)

Since man (the microcosm) is governed by the same force that rules the universe (the macrocosm), the "colic season" destroys more than a world of petals:

> Beginning with doom in the ghost, and in the springing marvels,
> Image of images, my metal phantom
> Forcing through the harebell,
> My man of leaves and the bronze root, mortal, unmortal. (p. 40)

The "metal" is "mortal" and, therefore, corruptible. Apparently, the "ghost" is not corruptible; yet it is not spoken of as immortal but as "unmortal." This odd coinage of Thomas is similar to his use of "undead" (p. 79). This term borrowed from Thomas' reading of Dracula means a kind of living dead.[15] Clearly, the "ghost" cannot be identified with the Christian concept of a personalized and individualized immortal soul. Indeed, Thomas makes it perfectly clear in the last stanza of this poem that the "ghost" is merely the presence of the life-death force ("the god of beginning"—Cadaver) in this temporary locus, man:

> Man was Cadaver's masker, the harnassing mantle,
> Windily master of man was the rotton fathom,
> My ghost in his metal neptune
> Forged in man's mineral.
> This was the god of beginning in the intricate seawhirl,
> And my images roared and rose on heaven's hill. (p. 44)

[14] See below, pp. 53-54, where Thomas' employment of such terms in describing man is discussed.

[15] Tindall, *A Reader's Guide*, p. 23, supplies this bit of information.

The last line seems inappropriate in this poem. William York Tindall says that "the triumph" of the images "is less actual than resolved upon and prayed for. There they are on heaven's hill; but the poet's 'thirtieth year to heaven' is not yet here—not by a long shot." [16]

The paradoxical character of Thomas' attitude toward death is best expressed by William T. Moynihan:

There is neither rest nor peace in his vision of death, there is rather an alleluia of all the earth's potential energy. . . . It is a matter of ultimate dread and loathing at one extreme . . . and a refusal to admit death, a mysticism of perpetuity at the other extreme.[17]

One would guess that it is this "mysticism of perpetuity" which Thomas trumpets so triumphantly in "Death Shall Have No Dominion." Although Thomas borrows St. Paul's words (Rom. 6:9) for the motif of his poem, he writes a hymn more to the indestructibility of matter than to faith in personal resurrection:

> Heads of the characters hammer through daisies;
> Break in the sun till the sun breaks down,
> And death shall have no dominion. (p. 77)

One surmises that this poem, too, represents more hope than conviction, that Thomas had a long journey to make before he could give the consent of faith to this statement. It is certainly true that the "dread and loathing" of death is the far more dominant theme of the early poems.

The following stanza from "When Once the Twilight Locks No Longer" (pp. 4-5) gives a "vulture's eye" view of Thomas' early universe. Most of his staple of horrors is gathered here: the womb as a tomb; the man-eating cancer; the rheumy, blinded eye; the blood and decay; the flies that live on garbage heaps:

> All issue armoured, of the grave,
> The redhaired cancer still alive,
> The cataracted eyes that filmed their cloth;

[16] Ibid., p. 86.
[17] William T. Moynihan, The Craft and Art of Dylan Thomas.

Some dead undid their bushy jaws,
And bags of blood let out their flies;
He had by heart the Christ-cross-row of death. (p. 4)

If in Hamlet "something is rotten in the state of Denmark"
(I, v, 90), in Thomas' early poetry there is something rotten in
the universe. It is old age growing into the bones of youth; it
is the stink of decay which exudes from the very sea of life; it is
the worm that never dies which eats at "the quick" (a pun here
upon both the sensitive area of skin under the fingernail and all
the living):

An old man's shank one-marrowed with my bone,
And all the herrings smelling in the sea,
I sit and watch the worm beneath my nail
Wearing the quick away. (p. 14)

Thomas struck a positive note when he declaimed "Man be my
metaphor" (p. 15), but he was unable to maintain this position
for long. In a later poem, he retracted these words and replaced
them with the ominous judgment that "Death is all metaphors"
(p. 80). Thomas was not exaggerating when he made this statement, nor was his imagination unequal to the task of supporting
it. He created a varied assortment of metaphors for death, although, in the manner of a madman, he has an obsession for
using them repeatedly. Perhaps, the maggot, with its connotation
of filth and decay is used most frequently in the early poems. The
following are a representative sampling:

"Man in his maggot's barren" (p. 3)

"I smelt the maggot in my stool." (p. 9)

"The root of tongues ends in a spentout cancer,
That but a name, where maggots have their X." (p. 25)

"The maggot that no man can kill." (p. 75)

The worm is more useful to Thomas the grave digger than to
Thomas the fisherman, and it is used almost as often as the maggot as a symbol of death:

"I sit and watch the worm beneath my nail
Wearing the quick away." (p. 14)

"And I am dumb to tell the lover's tomb
How at my sheet goes the same crooked worm." (p. 10)

"The corpse's lover, skinny as sin." (p. 38)

". . . the worms
Tell, if at all, the winter's storms
Or the funeral of the sun;" (p. 53)

Thomas' catalogue of death was not exhausted by the maggot and the worm. The following grouping of metaphors gives some indication of his range and variety. The months and seasons, particularly October and winter are frequently in evidence. In one poem, the trees and land are described as barren, and only the sturdy turnip is capable of weathering the deathly breath of the October wind; (p. 19) in another poem, "the town below lay leaved in October blood." (p. 115) The very air is unwholesome and "contages" all things. (p. 23) There are no end of birds, animals and nameless insects which make their ugly presence felt. The "scythe-eyed raven" (p. 39) darkens many poems; wild pigs (p. 35) recall the stench of death; adders braiding in the hair (p. 35) remind us of the death-giving glance of Medusa. The absurd world of the self-enclosed process appropriately ends in a cipher, the void, the empty circle, the "virgin o." (p. 21)

Time, death's agent, abets death in bringing man low. The disguises of time are too varied and the references to time too numerous to be completely explored in this chapter. The following metaphors of time are choice samplings of the poet's preoccupation with this theme. Time is a giant sponge that turns damp to dry, life to death; a leech that sucks out the vital fluids from the fount of life; a grave that leaks its contents as it chases its victim around the cinder track of the process; dressed in the royal robes of an ancient Egyptian, time may appear more amiable, but it is no less menacing; whatever the disguise, Time is essentially a murderer;

The mouth of time sucked, like a sponge
The milky acid on each hinge,
And swallowed dry the waters of the breast. (p. 4)

The lips of time leech to the fountain head; (p. 10)

When like a running grave time tracks you down (p. 22)

So fast I move defying time, the quiet gentleman
Whose beard wags in Egyptian wind. (p. 72)

Time kills me terribly. (p. 79)

The futility of life and the dread of death left Thomas in a continual muddle. Like Hamlet, whom he resembles in so many ways, Thomas walks through these early poems dressed in black, and his imagination suits his dress for it is "as foul/As Vulcan's Stithy." (III, ii, 88-89) In the universe of his early poetry "the earth seems . . . a sterile promontory . . . it appear no other thing . . . than a foul and pestilent congregation of vapors." (II, ii, 310, 314) The barren, sterile quality of the world is stressed over and over again; it is indeed "an unweeded garden, that grows to seed" and leaves the viewer to utter Hamlet's complaint: "How weary, stale, flat, and unprofitable/Seem to me all the uses of this world!" (I, ii, 133-34) Thomas, too, at times seems close to wishing "that this too too solid flesh would melt;" (I, ii, 129) he, too, seems to raise the question whether it is better "to be or not to be." (III, i, 56) Under the pressure of all this Thomas too seems a bit mad, suffering from "distemper." (III, iv, 123) Thomas is especially like Hamlet in his indecisiveness. In discussing "If I Were Tickled by the Rub of Love," Elder Olson makes an interesting comparison between Thomas' hero (which is a mask for Thomas himself, the hero of all his poems) and Hamlet. While Olson finds him a simpler character than Hamlet, his problems are more complex. Hamlet was troubled by a particular decision, Thomas' character is troubled by a host of decisions. More importantly, Olson notes:

Hamlet never doubts, in his practical syllogisms, the moral major premise, but only the instantial minor; Thomas' character doubts both. Hamlet can at least act on impulse; this character has contradictory impulses.[18]

During the middle period of his poetry, Thomas was confronted with three major decisions which were necessary for his full acceptance of life in his final period. First, he had to decide to give up his morbid preoccupation with death. Secondly, he had to come out of his isolation and establish bonds of compassion with other men. Thirdly, he had to reconcile himself to the fact of war.

In analyzing Thomas' "dream poems," Ralph Maud reaches the conclusion that what Thomas fears about dreams is not their fanciful nature but their physical threat to his manhood. Discovering what he believes to be references to onanism and wet dreams in these poems, Maud concludes:

Sexual waste becomes the chief symbol for all the other waste of youth in the land of dreams. . . . Sexual waste, standing for all waste, is eqivalent to death in life: this is the essential significance of the three dream poems.[19]

In general, we would agree with Maud; but we believe that Thomas was chiefly fearful of the illusionary character of dreams, and we also believe that dreams were specifically symbols of spiritual waste. Thomas' "boys of summer" (p. 1) see no meaning in the act of sex because life has no meaning:

> We are the dark deniers, let us summon
> Death from a summer woman. (p. 2)

Barren in thought and desire from the beginning, they are barren in their end: "Man in his maggot's barren" (p. 3). What Thomas really fears is the barrenness of life without meaning. Sexual imagery is used as symbol here as it is used in so many of Thomas' poems, but it is essentially a symbol of spiritual waste and not merely physical waste.

[18] Olson, p. 40.

[19] Ralph Maud, *Entrances to Dylan Thomas' Poetry* ("Critical Essays in Modern Literature"; Pittsburgh: University of Pittsburgh Press, 1963), p. 79.

In "When Once the Twilight Locks no Longer," the newly-born ambassador of "god" is sent forth to earth. After holding a "little Sabbath with the sun" (p. 4), his eyes are closed by the night stars, and he dreams of death:

> But when the stars, assuming shape,
> Drew in his eyes the straws of sleep,
> He drowned his father's magics in a dream. (p. 4)
>
> . . . . . .
>
> By trick or chance he fell asleep
> And conjured up a carcass shape
> To rob me of my fluids in his heart. (p. 5)

This dream, presented in stanzas four and five (six stanzas long in the original manuscript version),[20] is capable of drying up the sources of life. Just as dreaming is an illusion compared to the waking world, so is death an illusion compared to life. Dreaming and thinking about death are two kinds of sleeping. The creator attempts to rescue his creature from his morbid preoccupation by summoning him to fruitful life activity in the real world:

> Awake, my sleeper, to the sun,
> A worker in the morning town. (p. 5)

The world is already old, and soon enough the night of death will come when no man can work:

> The fences of the light are down
> All but the briskest riders thrown,
> And worlds hang on the trees. (p. 5)

Commenting on the last line of this poem, Tindall highlights for us the choice which is offered to the poet:

Abandon your morbid concern with womb and tomb, the creator urges his creature at last. . . . New worlds for old . . . or poems hang, like apples of knowledge, on the alphabet trees of Christcross row. Fall, leave the Garden, and face the poet's Calvary, says he to himself. . . .

[20] *Ibid.*, p. 75.

. . . [Thomas'] subject, as usual, is himself as boy and poet, at once creator and creature, and severest critic. . . . His famous struggle towards the light began earlier than most think.[21]

This illusionary aspect of dreams is depicted even more clearly and the hortatory call to life is no less evident in "Our Eunuch Dreams." This poem, which is composed of four shortened or curtal sonnets, depicts both the night dreams of adolescence and the day dreams of the movie-goer as two kinds of sleeping. Like eunuchs, dreams are sterile. The real danger of dreams is emphatically stated as spiritual: the young boy's sexual musings and the false romance of the movie screen, both escapes from reality, empty the dreamer of any higher religious aspiration, symbolized in the poem by the chief mystery of Christianity—the resurrection of the dead:

> The dream has sucked the sleeper of his faith
> That shrouded men might marrow as they fly. (p. 17)

The poet rejects both these false worlds and stakes his faith in reality ("This is the world. Have faith," p. 17). Maturity ("flowering") comes only to the man who is bold enough to put away dreaming and adventure forth ("faring hearts") into the real world:

> For we shall be a shouter like the cock,
> Blowing the old dead back; our shots shall smack
> The image from the plates;
> And we shall be fit fellows for a life,
> And who remain shall flower as they love,
> Praise to our faring hearts. (pp. 17-18)

Thomas would like to shout triumphantly like the cock, but often he is only a cock-on-a-dunghill. He is a man full of resolve, but he finds it difficult to put that resolve into practice. As Tindall said of him: "For every step forward, Thomas took one step backward." [22] But during his middle period Thomas—despite diffi-

[21] Tindall, A Reader's Guide, p. 34.
[22] Ibid., p. 20.

culties, doubts, and hesitations—manages to take most of his steps forward. He does make progress.

He renews his resolve and tries to strike a delicate balance in "Foster the Light" (p. 69). He resolves to put aside the inner weathers of "A Process in the Weather of the Heart" (pp. 6-7) by fostering the light of external reality ("nor weather winds that blow not down the bone") and mastering the night. He refuses to serve death ("nor serve the snowman's brain"), but does not wish to neglect the subject altogether ("And father all, nor fail the fly-lord's acre"). And at the end of the poem, offers one of his first prayers to his maker for assistance in this resolve.

In a poem written shortly after this one, Thomas tells himself and us that

> I have longed to move away
> From the hissing of the spent lie
> And the old terrors' continual cry
> Growing more terrible each day
> Goes over the hill into the deep sea; (p. 73)

Critics are divided in their opinion of just what the poet wishes to move away from. Religious, social, or poetic conventions—anyone or all three together—would be justified explanations.[23] But the references to "the ghosts in the air/And ghostly echoes on paper" reecho the fear of death in the preceding lines, and seem to say that the old poetic conventions of darkness and death are "the spent lie." The poet, nevertheless, hesitates to walk new ground. Perhaps, the old conventions like a delayed action bomb still have energies, which may explode in any new poetic attempt and confuse his vision:

> I have longed to move away but am afraid;
> Some life, yet unspent, might explode
> Out of the old lie burning on the ground,
> And crackling into the air, leave me half-blind. (p. 73)

This interpretation of the poet's dilemma is supported by a letter to Vernon Watkins, written a year after (1936) this poem.

[23] *Ibid.*, pp. 116-17.

After speaking of his poetry as the only thing saving him from unhappiness, Thomas goes on to say:

But here again I'm not free; perhaps, as you said once, I should stop writing altogether for some time; now I'm almost afraid of all the once necessary artifices and obscurities, and can't for the life or the death of me, get any real liberation, and diffusion or dilution or anything, into the churning bulk of words; I seem more than ever, to be tightly packing away everything I have and know into a mad-doctor's bag, and then locking it up: all you can see is the bag, all you can know is that it's full to the clasp, all you can trust is that the invisible and intangible things packed away are—if they could only be seen and touched—worth quite a lot. . . . I don't fear . . . any cessation or drying up, any coming to the end, any (sentimentally speaking) putting out of the fires; what I do fear is an ingrowing, the impulse growing like a toenail into the artifice.[24]

He seems to enjoy some success in "Find Meat on Bones" (pp. 74-75), which is a dialogue between father and son. Apparently arriving at some independence by revolting against his father's angry but puritanical advice to avoid women and rebel against life and death:

> Disturb no winding-sheets, my son,
> But when the ladies are cold as stone
> Then hang a ram rose over the rags.
> Rebel against the blinding moon
> And the parliament of sky,
> The kingcrafts of the wicked sea,
> Autocracy of night and day,
> Dictatorship of sun. . . .

After some bitter experience with life in which "[his] heart is cracked across; [his] face is haggard in the glass," the son replies:

> I cannot murder, like a fool,
> Season and sunshine, grace and girl,
> Nor can I smother the sweet waking.

In his capitulation, the poet makes his first harmonious statement:

[24] *Dylan Thomas: Letters to Vernon Watkins*, pp. 25-26.

> Light and dark are no enemies
> But one companion.

Broadening his poetic subject matter and technique could only be accomplished by broadening himself as a person. Just as the poet was afraid of giving up his old poetic convention, so was he afraid of giving up his isolation from his fellowmen. Donne had declared in an often-quoted sermon that "no man is an island"; but Thomas is not so sure that he shouldn't be:

> Ears in the island hear
> The wind pass like a fire,
> Eyes in this island see
> Ships anchor off the bay.
> Shall I run to the ships
> With the wind in my hair,
> Or stay till the day I die
> And welcome no sailor?
> Ships, hold you poison or grapes? (p. 67)

Undoubtedly, the death of his aunt, Annie Jones, awakened a deep compassion in him for the fates of all men. His love and admiration for this old lady and the life she lived so courageously shook the young poet free from his morbid self-preoccupation:

> Shakes a desolate boy who slits his throat
> In the dark of the coffin and sheds dry leaves,
> That breaks one bone to light with a judgment clout,
> After the feast of tear-stuffed time and thistles
> In a room with a stuffed fox and a stale fern. . . . (p. 96)

Not only Annie Jones, but the poet himself had lived in a room with dead things, "a stuffed fox and a stale fern." Her going to light is another summons to the poet, who resolves to

> Storm me forever over her grave until
> The stuffed lung of the fox twitch and cry Love
> And the strutting fern lay seeds on the black sill. (p. 97)

Thomas himself commented on the significance of this poem for his own personal and poetic development:

. . . The only one I have written that is, directly, about the life and death of one particular human being I knew—and not about the very many lives and deaths whether seen, as in my first poems, in the tumultous world of my own being or, as in the later poems, in war, grief, and the great holes and corners of universal love.[25]

Ironically, it was the Second World War which provided the greatest spur to the poet's development. Bitter and shocked about the war, Thomas tried to organize other writers in protest. He thought of registering as a conscientious objector. As it finally eventuated when he was called before the medical board, he was rejected as an acute asthmatic, unsuitable for fighting.[26] He did, however, serve as an air-raid warden; and this experience developed his compassion for the strangers from whom he had so long kept apart. As William T. Moynihan acutely observed: "Thomas finds the knowledge of death more deadening than the fact of death."[27] The war confronted Thomas with the fact of death; he faced it and matured. He speaks of this change in himself in the following poetic words:

> O you who could not cry
> On to the ground when a man died
> Put a tear for joy in the unearthly flood
> And laid your cheek against a cloud-formed shell: (p. 139)

. . . .

Now break a giant tear for the little known fall,

> For the drooping of homes
> That did not nurse our bones,
> Brave deaths of only ones never found,
> Now see, alone in us,
> Our own true strangers' dust
> Ride through the doors of our unentered house.
> Exiled in us we arouse the soft,
> Unclenched, armless, silk and rough love that breaks
> all rocks. (p. 140)

[25] Thomas, *Quite Early. . .* , pp. 174-175.
[26] Bill Read, *The Days of Dylan Thomas* (New York: McGraw-Hill, 1964), pp. 100-102.
[27] Moynihan, p. 234.

This change brought about in Thomas by World War II is almost identical with the change brought about in Wilfred Owen by World War I. The following excerpt from a sympathetic and acutely perceptive tribute which Thomas paid to Owen sums up this change:

There is no difference. Only the world has happened to him. And everything, as Yeats once said, happens in a blaze of light.[28]

In his final period, Thomas came not only to a full celebration of life and fertility, but also to a courageous and peaceful acceptance of death. In 1950, he was preparing a long poem to be called "In Country Heaven"; unfortunately, he only completed three poems, which were to form separate parts of the whole, before death took him. Thomas did grandly spell out, however, what he intended to do in this poem; and his words enable us to vividly imagine what it could have been:

What can I say about this long poem-to-be except that the plan of it is grand and simple and that the grandeur will seem, to many, to be purple and grandiose and the simplicity crude and sentimental? . . . The godhead. . . . He, on top of a hill in Heaven, weeps whenever, outside that state of being called his country, one of his worlds drops dead. . . . The Earth has killed itself. . . . And, one by one, these heavenly hedgerow men, who once were of Earth, call one another, through the long night, light and His tears falling, what they remember. . . . They remember places, fears, loves, exultation, misery, animal joy, ignorance and mysteries, all *we* know and do not know.

The poem is made of these tellings. And the poem becomes, at least, an affirmation of the beautiful and terrible worth of the Earth. It grows into a praise of what is and what could be on this lump in the skies. It is a poem about happiness.[29]

The three poems which Thomas completed are "In Country Sleep," "Over Sir John's Hill," and "In the White Giant's Thigh." We shall treat of "In Country Sleep" in Chapter Four. "Over Sir

[28] Thomas, *Quite Early. . .* , p. 123.
[29] *Ibid.*, pp. 179-80.

John's Hill" reveals that Thomas has come to accept death in the scheme of things even as he grieves the loss of life. Thomas is the chanter and the "sainted heron" is his priest in this, another of his ritual celebrations:

All praise of the hawk on fire in hawk-eyed dusk be sung,
When his viperish fuse hangs looped with flames under the brand
Wing, and blest shall
Young
Green chickens of the bay and bushes cluck, "dilly dally,
Come let us die."
We grieve as the blithe birds, never again, leave shingle and elm,
The heron and I,
I young Aesop fabling to the near night by the dingle
Of eels, saint heron hymning in the shell-hung distant
Crystal harbour vale . . . (p. 188)

Of more interest for our purposes is "In the White Giant's Thigh." This magical but mysterious title refers to a legendary carving on a Welsh cliff face. Perhaps going back to druidical rites, the white giant was a fertility icon among the Welsh from time immemorial. Barren girls would go to this hilltop and wait expectantly for lusty young men to fulfill their wishes.[30] The poem, an elegy, recreates and celebrates those girls and those days. They failed in their efforts to outwit time and death, but the poet loves them for their efforts and believes they live still:

(But nothing bore, no mouthing babe to the veined hives
Hugged, and barren and bare on Mother Goose's ground
They with the simple Jacks were a boulder of wives)—

Now curlew cry me down to kiss the mouths of their dust.
. . . .
Hale dead and deathless do the women of the hill
Love for ever meridian through the courters' trees
And the daughters of darkness flame like Fawkes fire still. (p. 199)

This celebration of fertility is a far cry from earlier Thomas of the womb-tomb period. All that he could think then was that "the

[30] Tindall in *A Reader's Guide,* pp. 292-93, supplies this bit of information which he received from Thomas himself.

womb/Drives in a death as life leaks out" (p. 6), and birth was described appropriately in this context as "the antiseptic funeral" (p. 42). In "A Saint About to Fall," a poem that honors the birth of his first son, the poet is for the most part fearful for this child born into a terrible world at war: ". . . agony has another mouth to feed" (p. 106). But the poem changes in tone at the end, and heralds a change in Thomas' attitude toward birth:

Cry joy that this witchlike midwife second
Bullies into rough seas you so gentle
And makes with a flick of the thumb and sun
A thundering bullring of your silent and girl-circled island (p. 107)

"If My Head Hurt a Hair's Foot," a dialogue between an unborn child and its mother, a similar note is struck at the end. The foetus has been telling his mother that she should abort him if he causes her any inconvenience. Although his mother bluntly denies his pleas, she is fearfully tormented about what the child might have to suffer in life:

Now to awake husked of gestures and my joy like a cave
To the anguish and carrion, to the infant forever unfree,
O my lost love bounced from a good home; (p. 109)

At the close of the poem, nevertheless, she is hopeful for what the miracle of birth has to offer:

The grave and my calm body are shut to your coming as stone,
And the endless beginning of prodigies suffers open. (p. 109)

Nowhere in Thomas' poetry, however, can his changing attitude toward time and death be seen so clearly as in the three poems which he wrote for his own birthday.[31] An examination of the individual volumes of Thomas' poetry shows that a birthday poem appeared in every volume except his second. This preoccupation with the same subject over a period of seventeen years is obviously very significant. What other day is so innately suit-

[31] Tindall, *A Reader's Guide*, p. 175, includes "Especially When the October Wind" among the birthday poems although he admits it is not typical.

able as a stopping off point to take stock of one's life than one's birthday?

In "Twenty-Four Years" (p. 110), Thomas views himself—half pityingly, half ironically—as a cocky young man all decked out on his way to town. He knows that his final destination will be "the elementary town" of death, but this is not news. He knew this when he sat in the womb "crouched like a tailor/Sewing a shroud for a journey." If the poet has a fear of death, which the tone of the entire poem intimates, he attempts to brazen it out by his "sensual strut" and flaunt death by enjoying himself while he can.

One is completely unprepared for Thomas' change of attitude only six years later. In "Poem in October," there is light not only in the loosening of rhythm, but also in image and idea. This October makes a sharp contrast with the October of "Especially When the October Wind" (pp. 19-20). There is no punishment from the frosty cold; no deadly ravens in bare trees; no hardy turnip in an otherwise fruitless land. This October is as "summery" (p. 113) as the tone of the whole poem. The sky is full of larks and the bushes are "brimming with whistling/Blackbirds" (p. 113). The land is fruitful "with apples/Pears and red currants" (p. 114). Only one line (the fourth from the last) is reminiscent of the bleak thoughts and season of the other poem: ". . . the town below layed leaved in October blood"(p. 115). Although this is true of the town, the poet's heart is as high as the hill he stands upon singing his "heart's truth" (p. 115).

This changed view of the season can be explained only by a change of season in the heart of the poet. The change is evident from the first line: "It was my thirtieth year to heaven" (p. 113), which stands in striking contrast to "twenty-four years remind the tears of my eyes" (p. 110). The religious imagery suggested by the word "heaven" is sustained throughout the poem in such phrases as "heron/Priested shore," "water praying," "the sea wet church," "parables/Of sunlight," "legends of the green chapels," and "the mystery/Sang alive." This religious turn of mind is associated with a return to childhood, and this theme shall be taken up in the next chapter.

"Poem on His Birthday," written when Thomas was thirty-five, opens with mixed emotions about his life, but closes with a burst of triumphant faith and joy. From his high-stilted boathouse on the Taf Estuary, Laughanre, where he watches the sea birds "work at their way to death" and hears the bell-buoys ring out life and death, the poet "celebrates and spurns/His driftwood thirty-fifth wind turned age." As he hears the bells toll, he seems to sense that his own death is imminent; yet, again, in contradictory fashion "he sings towards his anguish" (p. 190).

The poet recognizes that "dark is a way" and "a long way"; the mystery of life will never be fully solved by man on this earth. No man knows what the next day holds in store for him because "tomorrow weeps in a blind cage." This uncertainty which produces "terror" in man will remain until

> . . . chains break to a hammer flame
> And love unbolts the dark
>
> And freely he goes lost
> In the unknown, famous light of great
> And fabulous, dear God. (p. 191)

The word "fabulous" with its double connotation of fable and marvel is, perhaps, an indication that Thomas is still "doubting Thomas"; but this poem, as we have seen in two cases above, thrives on contradictory attitudes.

Certainly there is a remarkable change of view about life and death in this poem. The poet implies that temporal life imprisons or enchains a man. Only the hammer flame of God's love can break the chains and lead man out of the dark. "Light is a place" —the end of the journey, a stopping point and resting place. The poet can happily conceive of himself as a chanter in heaven's choir:

> With blessed, unborn God and His Ghost,
> And every soul His priest,
> Gulled and chanter in young Heaven's fold
> Be at cloud quaking peace. . . . (p. 192)

While the poet mourns "the voyage to ruin[he]must run," still he counts his blessings. One of them surely is that he no longer thinks of man as "unmortal" or "undead", but as "a spirit in love." Of all his blessings, he counts faith as the greatest:

> And this last blessing most,
>
> That the closer I move
> To death, one man through his sundered hulks,
>   The louder the sun blooms
> And the tusked, ramshackling sea exults;
>   And every wave of the way
> And gale I tackle, the whole world then,
>   With more triumphant faith
> Than ever was since the world was said,
>   Spins its morning of praise . . . (p. 193)

IV

FROM SIN TO INNOCENCE

"All-hollowed man wept for his white apparel"

In appraising the nature of Dylan Thomas' "god," Stuart Holroyd observes a notable lack of any sense of morality: "Indeed, Thomas' religious attitude may be compared with that of primitive man in the ages before moral concepts became associated with religion."[1] William Arrowsmith made a similar comment when he described Thomas' Christ as amoral and the settings and subject of his poems as pre-moral.[2] David Aivaz seemed to confirm the above opinions when he stated that he could discover only two poems by Thomas that directly discussed morality, but he confutes the above opinions when he submits that Thomas' later poetry gives evidence that he was developing beyond the world of "process" towards a world that is "intrinisically moral."[3] Taking a lead given by Elder Olson, who described Thomas as "a poet of the internal moral workings of the soul,"[4] it is the contention of this chapter that, although Thomas' moral concern reveals itself most explicitly in his later poetry, moral concern is implicit in his poetry from the beginning.

What at times seems an amoral quality in his poetry is mainly the result of Thomas' inner confusion. As Elder Olson has, again, preceptively noted: "It is not that he does not make decisions; he makes them repeatedly in the early poems, but we remain unconvinced of their durability or of the possibilty of their realization."[5] Thomas' primitive and faulty metaphysics is the major

[1] "Dylan Thomas and the Religion of the Instrinctive Life." *A Casebook*, p. 142.
[2] "The Wisdom of Poetry." *Ibid.*, p. 100.
[3] "The Poetry of Dylan Thomas," in Tedlock, pp. 198-199.
[4] Olson, p. 33.
[5] *Ibid.*, p. 40.

cause of his cloudy moral judgment and the weathervane insta-
bility of his moral decisions. If God's existence is denied, or his
nature misunderstood; if man's freedom of choice is denied, no
moral judgment can be made nor would one be considered. It
should be at least implicitly apparent from the last chapter that
so long as Thomas conceived of the world in terms of "process,"
he was necessarily viewing it as pantheistic, mechanistic, and
deterministic.[6] God was not a transcendent creator—immanent in
the world, yet distinct from his creation—but merely a vital force
or energy at once creative and destructive, expressing itself in
different material forms:

> The force that drives the water through the rocks
> Drives my red blood; that dries the mouthing streams
> Turns mine to wax. (p. 10)

In other poems, Thomas becomes more specific about the
nature of this vital force. Occasionally it is conceived of as a
liquid:

> Life rose and spouted from the rolling seas,
> Burst in the roots, pumped from the earth and rock
> The secret oils that drive the grass. (p. 27)

Sometimes, in more mechanical terms, it is compared to an elec-
tric circuit as in "my fuses timed to charge his heart." (p. 4) At

---

[6] As the works of modern philosophers and theologians make clear, "process" philosophy does not necessarily lead to pantheism, mechanism, and
determinism. See Leslie Dewart, *The Future of Belief* (New York: Herder
and Herder, 1966), pp. 77-121; Hans Urs Von Balthasar, *A Theology of
History* (London: Geoffrey Chapman, Ltd., 1964), pp. 111-148; Christopher
F. Mooney, *Teilhard de Chardin and the Mystery of Christ* (New York:
Harper and Row, 1966), pp. 36-66.

Raymond J. Nogar, O.P. has demonstrated in *Evolutionism: Its Powers and
Limits* ("Compact Studies"; Washington, D.C.: The Thomist Press, 1964)
that there is, however, a kind of evolutionism which tries to establish itself
as "a cosmic law that explains the origins of all things, a law which repudiates
all that is absolute, firm and immutable and gives values only to events and
their history." (p. 37). In this case, a biological theory has become a
monistic, mechanistic, historicist, life-philosophy of the cosmos by an illogical leap. . ." (p. 38) from a biological fact to a universal cosmic law. This
is the kind of leap that Thomas took in his early proto-metaphysics of the
process.

other times, it is represented as a more human but no less ominous figure, "the cloud perched tailors' master with nerves for cotton." (p. 148) In this case, the master tailor guides the apprentice who sits "in the groin of the natural doorway . . . crouched like a tailor/Sewing a shroud for a journey" on the sea of life. (p. 110)

If there remains any doubt that Thomas concept of the "process" committed him to a mechanistic interpretation of man, the following array of imagery from the early poems should dispel it. Man's flesh is described as "flesh's armour," "molten form," "Egypt's armour," "ghost in metal," "armoured," and "forged in man's mineral"; man's muscle and bone is "motor muscle," "night-geared," and "ribbing metal"; man's blood is "chemic," "synthetic," and "brassy"; man's nerves are "wired to the skull," and "girdered"; man's brain is "celled and soldered"; even man's face is a "petrol face." [7] Man was not, therefore, a personal, free, and self-directing agent, but a mechanically constructed and determined form in the general process, distinguished from other forms only by a painful consciousness of his state.

This mechanistic concept of man in the process led logically to a deterministic philosophy of life. This can be seen most clearly in Thomas' treatment of sex. Everywhere he looks, he sees the sexual process going on. This is seen not only in the driest of the dry worlds, the sands:

> And yellow was the multiplying sand,
> Each golden grain spat life into its fellow (p. 24)

but also in his mechanical male and female who resemble the sands in this:

> Two sand grains together in bed. (p. 127)

Since man is a mechanism subject to the forces of the universe, he cannot enjoy a personal relationship with another human being. Love, therefore, is an illusion. Death uses "love for his

[7] The sequence of references to these quotations is as follows: flesh: pp. 8, 36, 40, 41, 44 - bone: pp. 33, 38 - heart: pp. 20, 38, 39 - nerves: pp. 11, 33 - brain: p. 28 - face: p. 42.

trick" (p. 23) to get human beings to "commit the dead nuisance." (p. 40)

In "All, All and All the Dry Worlds Lever," Thomas asserts that man as well as the rest of creation keeps the process turning by the act of sex. "Dry" is Thomas' private metaphor for death; "damp" is Thomas' private metaphor for life; the "lever"—quite different from that of Archimedes—is the penis, which turns dry to damp. Sex is the "natural parallel" to the creative and destructive process which Thomas saw all about him; and his mechanical man experiences it as "the stroke of mechanical flesh on mine." By declaring that "the loin is glory in a working pallor," he tries to convince himself that he attains some purpose in serving the process, "the working world". He further exhorts himself neither to fear the sinfulness of the sex act ("the flesh's lock and vice," where "vice" connotes both sin and coupling) nor the birth-death which proceeds from the womb ("the cage for the scythe-eyed raven") because the process demands and predetermines this:

> Know, O my bone, the jointed lever,
> Fear not the screws that turn the voice,
> And the face to the driven lover.

There is no use rebelling against this situation for "this is the fortune of mankind: the natural peril." It is unfortunate and perilous since it leads inevitably to death, but the penis is "masterless," and, as repugnant as the case might seem, there is "no death more natural."

Francis Scarfe, among other critics, observed that Thomas' "primitive metaphysics related in the last analysis to a sexual interpretation of the universe." [8] In seeking life's purpose, Thomas went back to life's origins, "the sensual root and sap," (p. 20) as he understood it. This is manifest in a poem about the creation of the universe, "In the Beginning," which not only borrows the opening words of *Genesis* from the Old Testament, but which also borrows the Christian concept of the Trinity from the New Testament. It begins magnificently and reverently:

[8] "Dylan Thomas: A Pioneer," *A Casebook*, p. 24.

> In the beginning was the three-pointed star,
> One smile of light across the empty face. (p. 27)

But in the lines that follow, Thomas "irreverently" conceives of the creative act of the one God and trinity of persons in terms of sexual creation through the penis:

> One bough of bone across the rooting air
> . . . . . .
> A three-eyed, red-eyed spark, blunt as a flower. (p. 27)

To say that Thomas was preoccupied with sex is not the same thing as saying that he was erotic. As Ralph Maud has shown, Thomas approached his subject with a clinical detachment achieved by a technique of "distancing," that is, by filtering the meaning through a distorted syntax, and by choosing metaphors and symbols that carry a sexual denotation, but which are considerably remote from immediate erotic connotations.[9] Indeed, as Francis Scarfe has observed, "the poems also contain some implied defenses of this sexuality, justification by the poet to society and his own conscience."[10] Choosing in his early poems to reason "from the know dark of the earth" (p. 164), he committed himself to darkness until he could make some sort of act of faith in the God of light. Perhaps he is only being brazen and self-sufficient when he asks, "who is my Saviour?" in an early poem "Do Not Father Me"; but he certainly is serious and fearful when he speaks at the end of "the grave sin-eater." (p. 55)

It is not the purpose of poetry to make moral judgments; nor is it our purpose to judge Thomas the man when we examine his treatment of sin in his poetry. As Elder Olson has so convincingly argued, the struggle between sin and innocence constitutes one of the major conflicts in his poetry.[11] When Thomas spoke of discovering an angel and a beast in himself and saw it his duty to subjugate the beast,[12] he was not making a mere rhetorical ges-

[9] Maud, pp. 91-94.
[10] *A Casebook*, p. 30.
[11] Olson, pp. 36-41, 50-52.
[12] See above p. 9.

ture(at least not in regard to the struggle in his poetry). Perhaps, Francis Scarfe (quoted above) is presumptuous in stating that Thomas was trying to justify himself to society; he was certainly correct in seeing Thomas' moral struggle with his conscience in his poetry. Thomas, who rebelled against the Welsh chapel, who satirized the "hell and brimstone" preachers in his short story "The Peaches," [13] was, nevertheless, branded by his puritanical upbringing. Caitlin, Thomas' wife, substantiates this when she declares in *Leftover Life to Kill:* "Though Dylan imagined himself completely emancipated from his family background, there was a very strong puritanical streak in him, that his friends never suspected." [14] Apparently, Dylan Thomas himself never suspected it until his life was nearly over. In *Dylan Thomas in America,* John Malcolm Brinnin reports that Thomas, just a few weeks before he died, admitted to a friend's accusation, as if discovering it for the first time, "I am a Puritan." [15]

Consequently, although Thomas in his early poems viewed man in mechanistic terms, masterless against the sex impulse—the natural analogue to his sexual interpretation of the universe—still his Puritan conscience never ceased reminding him of sin. He seems to doubt the existence of a personal God, yet is half afraid that he might some day appear before and be held accountable to "unknown fabulous dear God." (p. 191) When Thomas described the creation of the world, he saw "heaven and hell mixed as they spun." (p. 27) His own sense of sin seems equally mixed for "doubting Thomas." He cannot forsake biblical imagery or biblical themes, but he insists on a personal interpretation of them. Treating the Christian account of Original sin and the Fall of man in the Garden of Eden in "Incarnate Devil," he does not hold man accountable for the Fall, but attributes it to external agents:

> The wisemen tell me that the garden gods
> Twined good and evil on an Eastern tree (p. 46)

He is born into a world he never made, and he finds it a mixture

[13] Dylan Thomas, *Portrait of the Artist as a Young Dog* (New Directions Paperback, New York: New Directions, 1955), pp. 17-18.
[14] Contained in *A Casebook*, p. 248.
[15] Also contained in *A Casebook*, p. 219.

of good and evil. It is "half holy" (p. 46) because of his Manichean concept of two principles of good and evil which divide the
work of the universe among themselves. If God supplied the material for the round of earth, it was Satan, the "incarnate devil in a
talking snake" who "in the shaping-time the circle stung awake."
(p. 46) And so it is not strange when the Puritan in Thomas is
faced with sexual desires that he attributes them "to the devil in
his loin" (p. 13) and sees the world as "half the devil's and my
own." (p. 14)

Even in his later poetry, after he has made much progress
towards the light, we hear Thomas revert to the old theme that
there can be no such thing as morality in a deterministic universe.
In "This Side of Truth," he sees good and bad as merely two ways
of moving toward death. Man may try to distinguish between the
two, but these terms have no meaning in a world where:

> . . . All is undone
> Under the unminding skies,
> Of innocence and guilt
> Before you move to make
> One gesture of the heart or head, (p. 116)
>
> . . . .
> And the wicked wish
>
> . . . .
> Is cast before you move,
> And all your deeds and words,
> Each truth, each lie,
> Die in unjudging love. (p. 117)

The words "unjudging love" seem inappropriate here and, perhaps, are meant to be taken ironically: there is no judgment
because there is no one in the heavens to care ("the unminding
sky"). There is also the possibility that, for justification and some
consolation, Thomas may be reverting to his earlier Manichean
notion. In this case, just as it was the job of one principle to incite
to sin, it was the job of the other to forgive. In "Incarnate Devil,"
God is given a two-fold office: man's jailor in earth's prison and
an emperor who fiddles while the earth burns. Only by royal
decree does He forgive all before the final immolation:

And God walked there who was a fiddling warden
And played down pardon from heaven's hill. (p. 46)

Whatever the interpretation, Thomas' conscience is still troubled, for to him sex without love is terrible. As Tindall observes "for Thomas, no vampire or fury was so awful as sex." [16] Thomas both fears and desires sex; he is both "chaste and the chaser." (p. 21) Ultimately, he asks to be delivered from "the female, deadly, and male/Libidinous betrayal." (p. 127)

In "When Like a Running Grave," the poet presents a nightmarish image of a woman (like time, death's agent) chasing him about a racetrack (the process, the circular world), using her pubic hairs like Father-time's scythe to cut him down:

When like a running grave, Time tracks you down,
Your calm and cuddled is a scythe of hairs. (p. 21)

The poet prays his masters, "head and heart" (p. 21), for deliverance from this love-death. When he says:

Deliver me who, timid in my tribe,
Of love am barer than Cadaver's trap, (p. 21)

Is he merely lamenting adolescent inexperience of sex or is he mourning the meaningless of the act without love? Whatever the reason, he soon realizes that his plea for deliverance is useless because he is not master of himself. The corpse hiding in the "skull" (p. 22) as a pilot in an airdome ("Cadaver in the hanger") (p. 22) gives orders ("Tells the stick, 'fail'") (p. 22) to the cockpit that the joystick (penis) die—a sexual usage in the sixteenth century.[17] As long as sex is the instrument of death, the world is truly "kissproof" (p. 23) for love is impossible. Paradoxically, since at times Thomas has seemed to deny there is any moral order, Thomas associated sex with sin.[18] With "the nitric stain [sperm seed] on fork [loins] and face," he despairs of "faith

[16] Tindall, p. 72.
[17] Tindall, p. 35.
[18] Moynihan, p. 169.

in the maiden's slime"; yet he seems to feel partly responsible for breaking the hymen, the "entered honour" (p. 22). A sense of both disgust and guilt is conveyed by the phrase "shame and the deep dishonours." His sense of responsibility in the matter is even more explicit in the phrases "suffering my stain," and "the erected crime/For my tall turrets carry as your sin." Commenting on this last line, Tindall says that Thomas "suffers from or accepts his 'stain': perhaps sin, all guilt, or original sin." This sentiment of Thomas is reiterated in the phrase "all love's sinners."

The sex-sin-death dilemma, which haunts most of the poet's early and middle work, is definitively and appropriately resolved in a long (54 quatrains), late (1941) poem, "The Ballad of the Longlegged Bait." I agree with Olson that the theme of the poem is "that salvation must be won through the mortification of the flesh." [19] Significantly, for this journey from darkness to light, the poet makes another famous sea-voyage. It is also significant that the poet has put away the embryo's shroud-sail and sails out willingly and hopefully.

> Then goodbye to the fishermanned
> Boat with it anchor free and fast
> As a bird hooking over the sea,
> High and dry by the top of the mast
>
> Whispered the affectionate sand
> And the bulwarks of the dazzled quay.
> For my sake sail, and never look back,
> Said the looking land. (p. 166)

We can be sure that the "goodbye" was a true "God-be-with-you" which was uttered by his friends, the sand and the quay, surprised ("dazzled") as they were by this new moral resolve. The land attempted to bolster this resolve by warning him not to look back in curiosity or longing, as Lot's wife did, for the Sodom and Gomorrah he was leaving. Following its advice, the poet safely comes to rest at the end of the poem in a new land, where he stands alone and lost, yet exultant and expectant.

[19] Olson, p. 24.

> Land, land, land, nothing remains
> Of the pacing, famous sea but its speech
> And into its talkative seven tombs
> The anchor dives through the floors of a church.
>
> Good-bye, good luck, struck the sun and the moon,
> To the fisherman lost on the land,
> He stands alone at the door of his home,
> With his long-legged heart in his hand. (p. 176)

That he now favors "dry" to "damp" is quite a reversal for Thomas. The sands and land no longer stand for death, but for life, a place for steady footing and momentary peace. The sea, the dark-deadly waters of the womb-tomb period, no longer remains at the end of his voyage. The last line suggests the allegorical nature of this voyage. One's expectation is confirmed by the quatrains that come in between the opening and closing sections, which we have just cited. Olson classifies this poem as one of Thomas' "pseudo narrative" poems, that is, story and characters are only a guise to express the feelings of a single consciousness —Thomas on his long voyage home.[20]

Very early in the poem, we perceive that this is no ordinary fisherman or fishing trip. The bait he is using is a girl, the "long-legged bait" of the title:

> For we saw him throw to the swift flood
> A girl alive with his hooks through her lips. (p. 167)

The girl serves as a love feast for all manner of sea creatures from above and below the deeps: shearwater birds, the polar eagle, whales, octopus, dolphins, turtles:

> Are making under the green, laid veil
> The long-legged beautiful bait their wives.
> . . . . . .
> Huge weddings in the waves. (p. 169)

Until, finally, "the seal kissed her dead!" (p. 170) There follows "rejoicing for that drifting death," (*ibid*) and it becomes clear

[20] Olson, p. 44.

that the girl is a symbolic mask for the poet's fleshly desires, "Sin who had a woman's shape." (p. 171) The sea voyage is thus symbolic of the means of purification and salvation; the fisherman again renews his good-byes to the good old days:

> Goodbye always for the flesh is cast
> And the fisherman winds his reel
> With no more desire than a ghost. (p. 172)

In a prophetic vision—echoing St. Paul in Romans 5 and 6— the poet looks to the future restoration of all that time and death have taken away. If sin brought death into the world, with the destruction of sin, resurrection is assured:

> One by one in dust and shawl,
> Dry as echoes and insect-faced,
> His fathers cling to the hand of the girl
> And the dead hand leads the past,
>
> Leads them as children and as air
> On to the blindly tossing tops;
> The centuries throw back their hair
> And the old men sing from newborn lips. (p. 173)

And a new heaven and a new earth is born; the lost Eden is rediscovered for there is "a garden holding to her hand." (p. 174)

Nowhere is the search for innocence so openly and poignantly presented than in Dylan Thomas' search for and celebration of his lost childhood. Full-throated and jubilant expression of this theme is given utterance only in his later poetry, but even as early as 1935 we hear the painful cry, "All-hollowed man wept for his white apparel." (p. 44) It also seems significant that for twenty years Thomas carried in his wallet a newspaper clipping reporting his winning of the 220 yard dash at the age of twelve.[21] John Malcolm Brinnin, who reported this fact, also describes Dylan's countenance as he thoughtfully gazed at this clipping in a Washington bar before a recording session of his poetry at the Library of Congress:

[21] John Malcolm Brinnin, *Dylan Thomas in America* (Compass Book Edition, New York: the Viking Press, 1957), p. 46.

As he studied it somewhat sadly now, his affection for that very thin and very little boy seemed to have opened in a moment a world of nostalgia. Very carefully, he folded the clipping and inserted it into his wallet.[22]

Almost all Thomas' prose pieces in *Quite Early One Morning* that treat of childhood, in passing or at length, were written in 1945 or after. "Reminiscences of Childhood" rhapsodizes upon the wonders, fears, games, people and places of Thomas' youth, and closes with the magical line, "the memories of childhood have no order, and no end." [23] In this same collection there is, of course, the already classic, "A Child's Christmas in Wales," with its preposterous Mr. and Mrs. Prospero, its connoisseur's collection of aunts and uncles, and throughout its entirety the joy and innocence of childhood, white as the beloved snow. "A Story," which is not really a story at all but a narrative of the town's annual drinking bout, is told from a young boy's delighted and delightful point of view. "Quite Early One Morning," the title story, and "Holiday Memory" are told by young men, but the child's fresh way of seeing is there; and the dominant memory of the young man's holiday is irrepressible children at the beach:

But over all the beautiful beaches I remember most the children playing, boys and girls tumbling, moving jewels, who might never be happy again. And "happy as a sandboy" is true as the heat of the sun.[24]

Underlying this fearful surmise that happiness ends with childhood was the painful awareness of the changes that come with time and the losses that accompany death. The nostalgic search for his lost childhood, as well as the grim recognition that he could not go home again are most evident in Thomas' "Return Journey," a radio play. Written in 1947, the scene is Swansea, Wales after the airraids of World War II. The unidentified "narrator", who has come back after fourteen years in search of "young Thomas" [25] is clearly "old" Thomas. He gets a clue from a

[22] *Ibid.*, p. 40.
[23] Thomas, *Quite Early One Morning*, p. 11.
[24] *Ibid.*, p. 40.
[25] *Ibid.*, p. 70.

customer in the hotel bar, and he hurries down to where the Three Lamps used to stand. Ghostly voices recall "two-typewriter Thomas the ace new-dick" [26] who used to stand and drink with the best of them. On past the Evening Post building, where garrulous young men are drowned in a torrent of ideas; on past the Kardomah Cafe "razed to the snow, the voices of the coffee-drinkers . . . lost in the willynilly flying of the years and the flakes"; [27] finally, he comes to the school and meets an old schoolmaster:

Oh yes, yes I remember him well,
though I do not know if I would recognize him now:
nobody grows any younger, or better,
and boys grow into much the sort of men one would suppose.[28]

The school, now charred and changed, is as difficult to recognize as the lost boys. Looking at the remains of burned initials on the broken desks, the narrator recalls the roster of the dead. Now, journeying further into childhood, the narrator arrives at the seaside haunts of the strutting adolescent, and the promenademan recalls the lost boy for him, "Oh yes, I knew him well. I've known him by the thousands." [29] The last stop is his beloved Cwmdonkin Park, where "the wild boys innocent as strawberries" (C.P. 124) used to roam. The parkkeeper says, "O yes, I knew him well. I think he was happy all the time. I've known him by the thousands." As to what has become of him since then, the parkkeeper replied, "Dead . . . Dead . . . Dead . . . Dead . . . Dead . . . Dead." [30]

Only children are happy because they do not yet know of time and death. They seem to live in a world of their own, another country, reminiscent of the lost Eden. This country of childhood seems to be identified with the countryside, the world of nature with which the child so easily identifies. In one of his greatest lyrics "Fern Hill," Thomas tells us what it was like when he was

26 *Ibid.*, p. 76.
27 *Ibid.*, p. 79.
28 *Ibid.*, p. 80.
29 *Ibid.*, p. 85.
30 *Ibid.*, p. 88.

young and made long summer visits to his Aunt Annie Jones'
dairy farm in Llangain.

Now as I was young and easy under the apple boughs
About the lilting house and happy as the grass was green,
  The night above the dingle starry,
.   .   .   .
And honoured among wagons I was prince of the apple towns
And once below a time I lordly had the trees and leaves
   Trail with daisies and barley
  Down the rivers of the windfall light. (p. 178)

He reveals that to the child waking in the early morning during
those rare days, each day was like the first day of creation in the
Garden of Eden:

And then to awake, and the farm, like a wanderer white
With the dew, come back, the cock on his shoulder; it was all
   Shining, it was Adam and maiden,
    The sky gathered again
   And the sun grew round that very day.
So it must have been after the birth of the simple light
In the first, spinning place, the spellbound horses walking
      warm
   Out of the whinnying green stable
    On to the fields of praise. (p. 179)

He was a prince and his son Llewelyn is described as a "king of
your blue eyes/In the blinding country of youth." (p. 116) The
child creates a kingdom out of the things he sees; not only is his
vision dazzling, but its very brightness also blinds him to the
world of time and death—the other country. For his childrens'
sake, Thomas would like to hold back time, hold back the seasons
of Fall and Winter (symbols of death) and let them abide green
and golden in spring and summer. This is the theme of an early
poem "Hold Hard, These Ancient Minutes in the Cuckoo's
Mouth" (p. 53), where "ancient minutes" represents time and
death, and the "cuckoo" (a spring bird) represents life. As he
says so beautifully in a long lyric "In Country Sleep," written for
his daughter, Aeron:

> The country is holy: O bide in that country kind,
> > Know the green good,
> Under the prayer wheeling moon in the rosy wood
> Be shielded by chant and flower and gay may you
> Lie in grace. (p. 182-183)

But he knows that the children will grow older and put aside their fairy tales, although he urges them "Hold hard, my country children in the world of tales." (p. 58) As soon as they begin to question their world, they will be rudely awakened from sleep to the real world. The angel of time and death will appear and with a burning sword drive them forever from Eden. And they will wonder if such a world ever existed:

> Was there a time when dancers with their fiddles
> In children's circuses could stay their troubles?
> There was a time they could cry over books,
> But time has set its maggot on their track.
> Under the arc of the sky they are unsafe. (p. 59)

Time, which haunts almost every stanza of "Fern Hill" could afford to be kindly

> > Time let me play and be
> > Golden in the mercy of his means (p 178)

because he knew the moment would inevitably come when

> . . . the children green and golden
> > Follow him out of grace. (p. 179)

The word "grace" as used in "Fern Hill" and "In Country Sleep" does not seem to be identified—as Christians do—with God's life in the soul, but with an absence of knowledge of death and time, death's agent.

The country was holy and the child innocent as long as he could unconsciously identify himself with the world of nature and rejoice in its wonders. Consciousness is, thus, a curse, not a blessing. For with the growth of self-awareness, man both sees himself as distinct from the natural world, and also realizes the meaning-

less of the process in which he is caught up. The amazing thing is
that Thomas was still able to see through a child's eyes again. In
"Poem in October," not only does he recreate a child's vision of
the world, but he experiences it so intently that he seems to
identify with the very child he was:

And I saw in the turning so clearly a child's
Forgotten mornings when he walked with his mother
        Through the parables
          Of sun light
And the legends of the green chapels
    And the twice told fields of infancy
That his tears burned my cheeks and his heart moved in mine.
                                (pp 114-115)

William York Tindall [31] points out that in this return to childhood, although psychologists might call it a regression, Thomas
has come a long way out of darkness into light. (p. 184) Perhaps
it only remained for him to come out of "country sleep" into
"country heaven" in order to complete the journey.

[31] Tindall, p. 184.

V

FROM DOUBT TO FAITH

"These once blind eyes have breathed a wind of visions"

As has been shown above, death is an obvious and overwhelming problem, which overshadows the whole of Dylan Thomas' poetry. No less obvious is an intensive preoccupation with sex (Chapter IV) as a concrete embodiment of the creative-destructive process. It is not easy to determine whether the triumphant faith, which illuminates the later poems especially, is the result of having solved the above two problems or is the cause of their solving. It would seem that all three problems were carried together, worked together, and fought together, frequently in the same poem, and that whatever progress Thomas made was achieved by bringing them into a harmony.

This threefold conflict is perhaps most graphic in a poem analyzed earlier,[1] "If I Were Tickled by the Rub of Love." In his effort to come to grips with the meaning of life, the poet examines his fears and desires and asks whether there is anything worth celebrating: death, sex, religion?

> And what's the rub? Death's feather on the nerve?
> Your mouth, my love, the thistle in the kiss?
> My Jack of Christ born thorny on the tree?
> The words of death are dryer than his stiff,
> My wordy wounds are printed with your hair.
> I would be tickled by the rub that is:
> Man be my metaphor. (p. 15)

As Tindall points out, "the rub that is" is clearly "adult reality." [2]

[1] See above, p. 23.
[2] Tindall, p. 48.

67

It is this very aspect, the existential concern for "the rub that is," which distinguishes Thomas' poetry from that of most of his contemporaries. Thomas' poetry reeks with the smell of man searching, sorting out the certainties and uncertainties of his experience; his poetry gathers together and looks with unflinching gaze on the seeming contradictions and contraries of human existence. The construction of a poem through opposed images, ideas, and experiences was not, therefore, a pose with Thomas, but a necessity. Robert Horan summarizes the situation very neatly:

It is in an effort to bring diverse and almost uncontrollable poles of his observation and sympathy into the same poem, or into the same system of consciousness and value, that he strikes the fundamental problem of composition and experience. . . . It is in this sense that I feel his grasp of reality is more shocking, and correspondingly more sensitized, than those around him, who are trapped in the affluence of style, and whose main consideration is to appear only temporarily baffled by the destruction of their society.[3]

Because his poetry presents the undergoing search, rather than the position already taken, Thomas' poetry radiates as much heat of conflict as it does the light of discovery. Indeed, Thomas was a man baffled. In a note which prefaces the *Collected Poems*, Thomas freely admits the "crudities, doubts, and confusions," which they contain; but he is quick to add that they "are written for the love of Man and in praise of God, and I'd be a damn' fool if they weren't." (xiii) Of course, there are always those who claim that Thomas sang at the top of his voice so that he might not hear too clearly the sounds of his own doubt. Yet an examination of Dylan Thomas' poetry reveals that he progressed a long way from the "dark deniers" (p. 92) of his early poetry to discover himself among the "found" (p. 165) in one of his last poems. Thomas, himself, confirms this opinion in a statement introducing a reading of his own poems for the B.B.C. in 1949. After looking through some seventy odd poems of his, some of which he found "odd, indeed," he chose for his reading

[3] "In Defense of Dylan Thomas," in Tedlock, p. 140.

... a few of the ones that do move a little way towards the state and destination I imagine I intended to be theirs when, in small rooms in Wales, arrogantly and devotedly I began them. For I like to think that the poems most narrowly odd are among those I wrote earliest, and that the later poems are wider and deeper....[14]

It is the contention of this chapter that Thomas' self-appraisal of his work is well founded, and that the reason his poetry is less odd and deeper is his ultimate arrival at a solution to the meaningless circle of the process in his "spiral of ascension" (p. 158) to Christ, "the sudden Sun." (p. 165)

Since Thomas constructed a bridge of words for his journey from darkness to light, it would perhaps be profitable to examine the relationship between words and reality in his poetry. From his boyhood days Thomas played word games, "word obsessions," as his friend, Daniel Jones called them.[5] Thomas declares that his love for words was in his "syllabic blood" (p. 20) from the moment of his birth:

> And from the first declension of the flesh
> I learnt man's tongue, to twist the shapes of thoughts
> Into the stony idiom of the brain,
> To shade and knit anew the patch of words
> Left by the dead who, in their moonless acre,
> Need no word's warmth. (p. 25)

Words were warm and comforting; they helped to make life bearable and ward off death. Making a poem, a creative act, is a defiance of death. In "On No Work of Words", Thomas tells us that not to be able to write is a lamentable situation because to die as a poet, as well as to die as a man, is a twofold payment to death:

> To surrender now is to pay the expensive ogre twice. (p. 104)

Thomas' first two volumes of poetry were his book of Genesis, whether he is concerned with creating "world, child, or poem, the three analogues of the Word." [6]

---

[4] Thomas, *Quite Early One Morning*, p. 166.
[5] Tedlock, p. 17.
[6] Tindall, p. 59.

> In the beginning was the word, the word
> That from the solid bases of the light
> Abstracted all the letters of the void;
> And from the cloudy bases of the breath
> The word flowed up, translating to the heart
> First characters of birth and death. (p. 27)

Again we see Thomas' metaphysical and theological concern in searching out the meaning of life in its origins. Here "the word" is both Logos and poet, recognition is given to the parallels between divine creation and artistic creation. Thomas frequently identified himself with the Word made flesh because, like Jesus, the poet is also sacrificed:

> No tell-tale lover has an end more certain,
> All legends' sweethearts on a tree of stories,
> My cross of tales behind the fabulous curtain. (p. 48)

In other poems, Thomas identifies the act of creation with the shedding of blood: he speaks of his heart which "sheds the syllabic blood and drains her words" (p. 19) and he envisions himself as a "soldier stained with spilt words." (p. 56) Although the poet suffers the wound of words and is willing to die for them, there are moments when he has his doubts about the value of his sacrifice. In a letter written to Vernon Watkins in 1938, Thomas spoke of his apprehension that words were depriving him of an active participation in life:

At the moment I am in action, a person of words, and not as I should be; a person of words in action.[7]

Words which should liberate him by opening the door to reality might also become his jailor, shutting him up "in a tower of words". (p. 19) This condition is copiously illustrated throughout "Especially When the October Wind," (p. 19) where the poet sees and hears all creation in terms of words: not only "the wordy shapes of women" or "the star-gestured children," but also "the vowelled beeches," "the oaken voices," "the water's speeches," "the wagging clock" which "tells the hour's word" and "declaims

[7] Thomas, Letters. . . , p. 36.

the morning," while the ravens, those "dark-vowelled birds" speak of death. There is always the fear that words might come between the actual world and the people and things in it. This misgiving is clearly apparent in the following passage from "The Orchards," a short story:

The word is too much with us. He raised his pencil so that its shadow fell, a tower of wood and lead, on the clean paper; he fingered the pencil tower, the half-moon of his thumbnail rising and setting behind the leaden spire. The tower fell, down fell the city of words, the walls of a poem, the symmetrical letters. He marked the disintegration of the ciphers as the light failed, the sun drove down into a foremorning, and the word of the sea rolled over the sun. Image, all image, he cried to the fallen tower as the night came on, whose harp is the sea, whose burning candle is the sun? An image of man, he rose to his feet and drew the curtains open. Peach, like a simile, lay over the roofs of the town. Image, all image, cried Marlais.[9]

We see, therefore, that despite Thomas' statement in 1946 that "a good poem is a contribution to reality," [10] there was a time when he feared that art was illusion. This theme seems to be borne out in "Today This Insect." (p. 47) Although the poem is cryptic and allows for a variety of interpretations, the phrase, "fibs of vision," in the third stanza clearly refers to the fiction of art.[11] The same idea is repeated in such phrases as "the sweet lies plenty" and "the hollow words" of "Out of the Sighs" (p. 56) and "the sweetly blown trumpet of lies" of "O Make Me a Mask." (p. 94) Thomas, who seeks reality and loves poetry, finds himself tossed on the horns of a dilemma: at times he would like to dispense with questioning reality and forget the pain of life in art:

> Were that enough to ease the pain,
>
> . . . . . .
>
> Were vagueness enough and the sweet lies plenty,
> The hollow words could bear all suffering
> And cure me of ills (p. 56)

[9] Thomas, *Adventures in the Skin Trade and Other Stories* (New York: New Directions, 1964), pp. 140-141.
[10] Thomas, *Quite Early One Morning*, p. 192.
[11] Tindall, p. 91.

Again, this time borrowing the image of the young scamp from *Portrait of the Artist as a Young Dog*, he puts it another way:

Man should be cured of distemper (p. 57)

So long as poetry fails to provide answers to his fundamental questions, the poet is not cured, but remains disturbed, disordered, if not deranged. The only cure for the "madman" in him is reality. The poet can well remember being confounded before the mystery of the constructive-destructive process, of man's relationship to the universe, of the relationship of time and eternity. In "The Force that Through the Green Fuse Drives the Flower," five times he states that "I am dumb," that is unable to voice an explanation of these mysteries. The two closing lines are typical of this dumbfoundedness:

And I am dumb to tell the lover's tomb
How at my sheet goes the same crooked worm. (p. 10)

It is the opinion of David Aivaz that Thomas believed that "both art and faith . . . are illusionary when they deny process." [12] Perhaps it would be stated more accurately to say that art and faith are illusionary if they cease to take account of "process" or to offer an explanation that makes human life meaningful within the process.

William Moynihan has called attention to Thomas' use of rhetorical questioning to express doubt, confusion, dumbness.[13] Children are especially notable for raising questions that adults cannot answer: "The child shall question all his days." (pg. 62) Thomas, who as a young schoolboy received the advice from his mentors not to question but to be content, could not accept this solution:

I hear content, and "Be content"
Ring like a handbell through the corridors,
And "Know no answer," and I know
No answer to the children's cry (p. 62)

[12] Tedlock, p. 200.
[13] Moynihan, p. 190.

Over the years, he has received much advice on the matter—to be philosophical, to mistrust the brain and follow his emotions, to follow D. H. Lawrence's dictum that the knowledge of the blood is surest—but none of these ways have provided answers:

> I have been told to reason by the heart,
> But heart, like head, leads helplessly;
> I have been told to reason by the pulse,
> And, when it quickens, alter actions pace
>
> . . . .
> I have heard many years of telling,
> And many years should see some change. (p. 72)

But his two closing lines indicate that no solution has come to his problems; rather he is back with the innocent schoolboys in Cwmdonkin Park, waiting for answers to fall like balls from heaven:

> The ball I threw while playing in the park
> Has not yet reached the ground. (*Ibid.*)

Judging from an earlier poem, it would seem that the poet expects he will have a long wait, indeed, before the final answers come:

> Not till, from high and low, their dust
> Sprinkles in children's eyes a long-last sleep
> And dusk is crowded with the children's ghosts,
> Shall a white answer echo from the rooftops. (p. 62)

Certainly, final answers won't come to blind eyes "this side of truth," this side of the grave, but there is a definite implication that an answer is expected after death. We are reminded of these words written for his thirty-ninth birthday:

> And to-morrow weeps in a blind cage
> Terror will rage apart
> Before chains break to a hammer flame
> And love unbolts the dark. (p. 191)

"God is love" says St. John. Is it this God who will smite the chains and set the children free, which time had held captive so long?:

> Time held me green and dying
> Though I sang in my chains like the sea. (p. 180)

We will reserve an answer to that question for the last section of this chapter. We showed in Chapter III how much the victims of the air-raids, personal losses, marriage and children contributed to Thomas' acceptance of life over death. We hinted in Chapter IV and we would now attempt to demonstrate that human love was a step towards Thomas' acceptance of Divine Love.

Both Karl Shapiro (Casebook 173) and John Wain (Casebook 69) have noted (almost by way of censure) that Thomas has written hardly one good love poem; they contend that this stems from his being taken up with the process of sex to the exclusion of anything else. Although, as we have seen, Thomas sought purgation in his poetry from sex-sin, it is no less true that Thomas was preoccupied with the sexual process in much of his work. It is also true that he did not write any love poems in the tradition of the Romantics or neo-Romantics. The closest he comes to this tradition is in "In the White Giant's Thigh," where he celebrates the joys of physical love:

> Or, butter fat goosegirls, bounced in a gambo bed,
> Their breasts full of honey, under their gander king
> Trounced by his wings in the hissing shippen, long dead
> And gone that barley dark where their clogs danced in the spring
> And their firefly hairpins flew, and the ricks ran round ... (p. 198)

In this late poem, which praises fertility over barrenness, life over death, it is not surprising to find a marked absence of the puritanical Thomas and the disappearance of all the machinery of the physical process.

Accepting the fact that Thomas wrote no traditional love poetry, we should not ignore the equally important fact that his method of composition could not be considered traditional either. Granting the correctness of our thesis—that his principal preoccupations were philosophical, theological and moral—one might again expect an absence of the traditional love lyric. It does not follow, however, that Thomas did not write of love, did not get beyond the sexual act. In "And Death Shall Have No Dominion," Thomas confidently declares: "Though lovers be lost love shall not." (p. 77) Perhaps, rather surprisingly, this reflection is reiterated in a prayer to the aforementioned "goosegirls" that they:

> Teach me the love that is evergreen after the fall leaved
> Grave. . . . (p. 199)

We are not trying to beg the question by choosing quotations that smack more of the mystic than the hedonist. Even in those poems which clearly are concerned with his marriage to Caitlin—stormy and tempestuous as it proved to be at times—Thomas reveals in flashes a mystical cast of thought.[14] Witness, for example, the following line from a poem which begins "in a warring absense" (p. 87) and ends "in a forgiving presence": (p. 89)

These once-blind eyes have breathed a wind of visions. (p. 89) In another, somewhat obscure, marriage poem, "Unluckily for a Death"—originally entitled "Poem (for Caitlin)"—Thomas seems to say that "spiritual" love can be reached, made believable and understandable, through "natural love": [15]

> Love, my fate got luckily,
> Teaches with no telling
> That the phoenix' bid for heaven and the desire after
> Death in the carved nunnery
> Both shall fail if I bow not to your blessing
> Nor walk in the cool of your mortal garden
> With immortality at my side like Christ the sky. (p. 121)

The paridisal allusion to the poet as Adam or God walking in the cool of a mortal Eden, prepares for the biblical allusion to the newly created world in the clear and magnificent last lines:

[14] See Jacob Korg, "The Rhetoric of Mysticism," *Dylan Thomas* ("Twayne's English Author Series," New York: Twayne Publishers, Inc., 1965), pp. 26-55.

[15] Derek Stanford, *Dylan Thomas—A Literary Study* (Paperbound Edition, New York: The Citadel Press, 1964), p. 123.

> . . . my true love, hold me.
> In your every inch and glance is the globe of genesis spun
> And the living earth your sons. (p. 122)

The transition from human love to divine love is best substanti-
ated by two poems in which Thomas introduces a strange seraph-
like creature (partly woman, partly angel) which he designates
as a "she-bird." The vision and language of love, which we have
already seen were soaked in biblical imagery, become increasingly mystic.

The asylum mentioned in "Love in the Asylum" represents
refuge as well as madhouse; [16] in either case, it is an appropriate
place for a poet who has claimed to hold a madman in him and
who has found it so difficult to come out of the dark. It is fitting
also that the girl he admits to his room is "a girl mad as birds."
Her madness seems less that of insanity and more that divine
madness of the seer, for she shuts out darkness and brings a
divine light (knowledge) to the house previously closed to
heaven:

> Bolting the night of the door with her arm her plume.
>   Strait in the mazed bed
> She deludes the heaven-proof house with entering clouds
>
> . . . . .
> She has come possessed
> Who admits the delusive light through the bouncing wall,
>   Possessed by the skies
>
> . . . . .
> And taken by light in her arms at long and dear last
>   I may without fail
> Suffer the first vision that set fire to the stars. (p. 119)

The patently mythical character of the long, narrative poem,
"A Winter's Tale," provides further justification for an allegorical
interpretation of the "she-bird." Instead of an asylum, our man is
in a farmhouse this time; it is mid-winter and he is alone. The
poet stresses this isolation by calling the cabin a "firelit island,"
(p. 131) the only bit of warmth against the freezing and barren
snow which surrounds him. "The cup and the cut bread," remi-

[16] Tindall, p. 191.

niscent of the Eucharistic banquet of the Last Supper, fore-
shadow the love feast being prepared for this man "at the point
of love, forsaken and afraid." (p. 132) The man kneels "on the
cold stones" and his love hunger ascends to "the home of prayers/
and fires," and this was his prayer:

> Deliver him, he cried,
> By losing him all in love, and cast his need
> Alone and naked in the engulfing bride,
> Never to flourish in the fields of the white seed
> Or flower under the time dying flesh astride. (p. 133)

This love death aspiration is not unlike the prayers uttered by
such great mystics as St. John of the Cross and St. Teresa of
Avila. We shall note the spiritual connotation which, in the context of the poem, Thomas conveys through deftly contrasted
images of fire and cold, light and dark.

His prayer has been heard, and

> . . . the bride bed forever sought
> By the believer lost and the hurled outcast of light (p. 133)

is being prepared. Mysteriously, the "dark door" of the farmhouse opens wide, and the man saw "a she-bird rose and rayed
like a burning bridge." (p. 134) Her very presence transforms
the world around her; she brings spring in winter, life in death:
"The dead oak walks for love." (p. 134) Charmed by her voice, the
man fled from the warm comfort of his house, and "he ran like
the wind after the kindling flight." (p. 135) The man chases
through the cold all night long until finally the "she-bird" alights
and welcomes him:

> And the wings glided wide and he was hymned and wedded,
> And through the thighs of the engulfing bride,
> The woman breasted and the heaven headed

> Bird, he was brought low,
> Burning in the bride bed of love, in the whirl—
> Pool at the wanting center in the folds
> Of Paradise, in the spun bud of the world
> And she rose with him flowering in her melting snow. (p. 137)

This ecstatic union achieved in "mystical marriage" climaxes Thomas' long search for unity and prepares the way for the majestic act of faith made in "Vision and Prayer" and "Poem on His Birthday." Commenting on Thomas' mystical tendency, E. Glyn Lewis calls attention to the attraction that "Cosmic unity" had for the poet.[17] Thomas expresses this viewpoint in the following passage from his short story, "The Orchards":

It is all one, the loud voice and the still voice striking a common silence, the dowdy lady flattening her nose against the panes, and the well-mourned lady. The word is too much with, and the dead word. It is all one, the rain and the macadam; it is all one, the hail and the cinder, the flesh and the rough dust. High above the hum of the houses, far from the sky and the frozen fence, he questioned each shadow; man among ghosts, and ghosts in clover, he moved for the last answer.[18]

We find additional support for this idea of "oneness" in such poems as: "From Love's First Fever to Her Plague," (p. 24) where Thomas speaks of the oneness of things before birth; "In the Beginning" (p. 27) where he speaks of the oneness of things before creation; and "We Lying by Seasand," where the poet expresses a desire that "the dry tide-master," death

> Should cure our ills of the water
> With a one-colored calm. (p. 91)

But, as we have already indicated, Thomas sought more than a general cosmic unity; he aspired to a personal union with the creator of all things.

This aspiration is beautifully expressed in one of his earliest prayers:

> O who is glory in the shapeless maps,
> Now make the world of me as I have made
> A merry manshape of your walking circle. (p. 70)

[17] See "Dylan Thomas" in Tedlock, pp. 172-180.
[18] Thomas, Adventures. . . , p. 142.

Here Thomas prays to God, the "glory in the shapeless map" of the skies, that just as he, the poet, using man as his metaphor has shaped the world into a meaning, so, please God, may he be shaped, given a meaning. The word "created," as used in the above passage, should be understood as "re-created," or the continuing evolutionary process of death and rebirth.

The need and meaning of rebirth is specifically spoken of in "I Dreamed My Genesis," where the poet dreams "in sweat of sleep" (p. 33) his first birth, dies to this and is born again:

> And power was contagious in my birth, second
> Rise of the skeleton and
> Rerobing of the naked ghost. Manhood
> Spat up from the resuffered pain.
>
> I dreamed my genesis in sweat of death, fallen
> Twice in the feeding sea, grown
> Stale of Adam's brine, until, Vision
> of new man strength, I seek the sun. (p. 34)

Treating of the many references to "vision" in Thomas' poetry, David Aivaz observes:

> The function of vision is to point the way. . . . A revelation, it is expressed in images of revelation. The coming of vision is likened to the breaking of day.[19]

and again,

> In Thomas' later poems especially, vision seems not only to celebrate the process, but also to inform it.[20]

The concept introduced in the previous poem that redemptive suffering is necessary in order to become the "new man," [21] is repeated in "I Fellowed Sleep.":

[19] Tedlock, p. 201.
[20] *Ibid.*, p. 206.
[21] See I Cor. 15:45-49 when St. Paul speaks of putting off the old Adam and putting on the new man in Christ.

> Then all the matter of the living air
> Raised up a voice, and, clinging on the words,
> I spelt my vision with a hand and hair,
> How light the sleeping on this soily star
> How deep the waking in the worlded clouds.
>
> There grows the hour's ladder to the sun,
> Each rung a love or losing to the last,
> The inches monkeyed by the blood of man. (p. 32)

The nature of the vision is spelled out in these stanzas. In the phrase, "the hour's ladder to the sun," we get the first hint of "the spiral of ascension," (p. 158) that the poet was ultimately to accept as a solution of the meaningless circle of the process. Commenting on this phrase, Tindall observes:

> If sun is a pun on son, he will seek not only enlightenment and light of morning after a bad night, but Christ and his own identity as risen son.[22]

Moreover, Time is no longer the agent of death, but of life. It provides man with the opportunity of passage from a troubled sleep on this "soily star" of earth, to a profound awakening in the kingdom of the Son. The process is no longer a closed, mechanical circle, but a continuing evolutionary process; "the inches monkeyed by the blood of man." Since the rungs of ascent are "a love or losing," a spiritual evolution is clearly intended. In a later troubled poem written in troubled times, Thomas attempts to reassure himself about this spiritual discovery:

> Out of the sighs a little comes,
> But not of grief, for I have knocked down that
> Before the agony; the spirit grows,
> Forgets, and cries;
> A little comes, is tasted and found good;
> All could not disappoint;
> There must be praised some certainty,
> If not of loving well, then not,
> And that is true after perpetual defeat. (p. 56)

[22] Tindall, p. 70.

No discussion of Thomas' spiritual journey would be complete without, at least, mentioning the ten "Altarwise by Owl-light" sonnets (80-85) Generally considered one of Thomas' most obscure and difficult poems, there have been no end of explicators, we do not intend here to add our explication to the list. Two of the best are William York Tindall [23] and Elder Olson.[24] While they are in general agreement that Thomas is making another journey toward the light, they differ in their interpretation of the journey. According to Tindall, Thomas is only making a secular journey; according to Olson, a spiritual journey. The most intensive treatment of the sonnets to date is a study by H. H. Kleinman. The following words from his introduction show him in essential agreement with Olson that the journey is a spiritual one:

I believe the sonnets are a deeply moving statement of religious perplexity concluding in spiritual certainty. They reflect the wonder, awe, doubt, and faith of a young poet who could not reconcile the capacity of divine pity with the necessity of human sacrifice. The paradox of the Incarnation and Passion affected Dylan Thomas early in his career . . . The poem begins with a sonnet mocking the descent of the Word., it concludes in a spiraling ascent of faith.[25]

The fact that there is a disagreement between Tindall and the other two critics raises the final question to be treated in this chapter: What exactly is the nature of Thomas' "faith?" Is it merely natural or is it supernatural?

Stuart Holroyd claims that Thomas' god was not transcendent and personal, merely immanent, in fact, pantheistic.[26] He contends that Thomas had no metaphysical interests and declares that Thomas' religion was the religion of the instinctive life—the life of the unconscious:

[23] Tindall, pp. 126-143.
[24] Olson, pp. 63-89.
[25] H. H. Kleinman, *The Religious Sonnets of Dylan Thomas* ("Perspectives in Criticism" No. 13, Berkeley and Los Angeles: University of California Press, 1963), pp. 10-11.
[26] *A Casebook*, p. 143.

Thomas' darkness is not the darkness of God, but rather that darkness of the unconscious mind. Out of that darkness man emerges into consciousness, and when the brief span of his life is completed he returns to it. For what purpose he emerges and what he accomplishes during the period of consciousness, are questions the poet never asked.[27]

On the contrary, the entire argument of this paper has demonstrated that Thomas was constantly asking such questions; they were what his journey was all about. If Holroyd insists on equating Thomas' darkness with his unconscious, he could have made his argument a bit more tenable by basing it on Jungian psychology. According to Jung, man's sin in Genesis is a symbolic expression of man's breaking from the unconscious oneness with nature into individual consciousness. This was the Promethean act: eating of the tree of knowledge was the stealing of the holy fire of consciousness from the gods.[28] Given this interpretation, Thomas' dredging of the unconscious would at least be meaningful—self-awareness would be the light he came to. While we would contend that Thomas' journey took him much further than this, still he would have a kind of religion because Jung teaches that "the experience of finding the Self is redemption." [29]

While granting that Dylan Thomas did make progress toward the light (one would surmise that this is to be understood in a manner akin to Jung), William York Tindall refuses to believe that Thomas ever arrived at faith in a Christian God. This view weaves through his entire book, but finds most explicit expression in the statement that Thomas' faith "is a secular, not a theological, virtue." [30] Neither overlooking nor rejecting the biblical images in Thomas poetry, Tindall, nevertheless, maintains that they are merely used as metaphors, symbols or analogues for the comparable experience of holiness in nature. Tindall's display of enormous erudition and his sustained brilliance in explication,

---

[27] *Ibid.*, p. 145.

[28] Jacobi, p. 28.

[29] According to Joseph Goldbrunner, *Individuation—a Study of the Depth Psychology of Carl Gustav Jung* (Paperback edition., Notre Dame, Indiana: University of Notre Dame Press, 1964), p. 169.

[30] Tindall, p. 288.

both add tremendous weight to his opinion; and it would seem somewhat temerarious to quarrel with it. Nevertheless, we do; and we base our argument on Tindall's own words:

Jesus seems the light to which child, poet, and poem ascend. These seemings amount at last, like circumstantial evidence, to all but certainty.[31]

If this is the case, although certainty cannot be obtained for such an interpretation, neither can it be obtained against such an interpretation.

We would raise the question: Why did Thomas reject the nightmare universe of his early poems and construct one of pristine beauty and holiness in his later poetry? Since Nature cannot give meaning to itself, Thomas must have come to a new understanding of it. Furthermore, Thomas' use of biblical imagery in his later poems is radically different from the use in his early poems. Elder Olson argues along these same lines and concludes:

. . . He has recaptured, in the charming natural world of Wales, something of the lost Eden and something of a foretoken of Heaven. There is undoubtedly a development from doubt and fear to faith and hope, and the moving cause is love; he comes to love of God by learning to love man and the world of nature.[32]

Examining only the images of light and darkness in Thomas' poetry, Charles F. Knauber concludes that "the condition of light and dark represent particular aspects of experimental faith." [33] Knauber indicates that there are three distinct periods in Thomas' poetry. In the first, light and dark are treated at the completely sensory level, and the awareness of their significance is on no higher level than that of myth. Light and dark are here seen representing something larger than themselves, but the poet does not arrive at spiritual awareness of another world. Day and night,

---

[31] *Ibid.*, p. 242.

[32] Olson, p. 20.

[33] Charles F. Knauber, "Imagery of Light in Dylan Thomas," *Rennascence*, VI (Spring, 1954), p. 95.

together with the changing seasons and changing tides, constitute the chief source of this myth. In the second period, the poet shows an advance in knowledge, coupled with the imaginative power to express this knowledge vividly. This results in the transcending of commonplace reality. In this stage, the poet is able to abstract

from the essences of sensible dark . . . an idea of the darkness of a yonder place, interpreting it as a special and temporal dimension that can be physically traversed. Man motivated by the dream of vision and the restless passion of desire, is prompted to the heroic role.[34]

In the third period, this movement toward light is finally realized by the poet's act of faith in God, who gives meaning to all other light images.

This mention of God, who dwells in light ineffable, seems an appropriate preface to our final consideration—Thomas' acceptance of a personal God in "Vision and Prayer." This sequence of twelve poems is appropriately divided into two parts, each part containing six poems. An additional bit of circumstantial evidence for the sincerity of Thomas' conversion is obtained from his reverting to the emblematic shapes employed frequently by George Herbert, a religious "metaphysical poet." The diamond shapes given to the poems of part one are perhaps reminiscent of Hopkins' metaphor for Christ, the "immortal diamond." The shapes in part two can be variously interpreted as wings (which would suggest Herbert's "Easter Wings"), chalices, or hour-glasses —all of which would be, whether considered singly or collectively, present and operative.[35] In the first poem of the "Vision," the poet asks the identity of the child in the dark womb, being born in the room next to his own. In the next poem, the poet waits quietly ("still as stone": p. 155) behind the dividing wall, "thin as a Wren bone" (p. 155) for the child to be born to give an account of himself. Whoever the child is, he will be a child of light when he escapes the darkness of the womb:

[34] *Ibid.*, p. 96.
[35] Tindall, pp. 239-241.

> And the dark thrown
> From his loin
> To   bright
>   Light.   (p. 155)

In the third poem, the poet gets an intuition that the nativity
scene in which he is participating is none other than another Beth-
lehem. The child to be born is clearly Jesus, "the dazzler of
heaven." At this point, the poet is obviously fearful that this
turbulent birth will break not only the wren wall of the womb,
but the wren wall of the room where he is hiding in darkness. He
knows that if the light of the child touches him, he shall be
compelled, beyond all protest, to burn in the kiss of this child
"with a bonfire in His mouth."

> I   shall   run   lost   in   sudden
> Terror   and   shining   from
> The once hooded room
> Crying   in   vain
> In the caldron
> Of   his
>   Kiss   (p. 156)

What he fears will happen, does happen in the fourth poem:

> For I was lost who have come
> To dumbfounding haven
> And the finding one   (p. 157)

In the fifth and sixth poems, he has an apocalyptic vision of all
creation returning to the creator in a "spiral of ascension" (p.
158), and all the redeemed world offers homage as it did in the
first days of creation when

> The
> Born sea
> Praised the sun
> The finding one
> And upright Adam
> Sang   upon   origin!   (p. 150)

The whole world winds its way home to the great clock maker who wound the clock of time ("The world winding home!", *Ibid.*)

In the first poem of the second section of the poem, "Prayer," the lost-found poet prays for the sheep still lost in the country of death, those "who glory in the swinish plains of carrion" (p. 160) as he once did. He still feels fellowship with them, although he admits that

> . . . I belong
> Not wholly to that lamenting
> Brethren for joy has moved within
> The inmost marrow of my heart bone.   (p. 160)

His prayer is revealed in the third, fourth and fifth poems, and its contents is unexpected and paradoxical. The poet prays that the "finding one"

> . . . let the dead lie though they moan
> For his briared hands to hoist them
> To the shrine of his world's wound   (p. 162)

What the poet seems to be thinking is that as Christ, "the world's wound," has demonstrated, spiritual rebirth requires the painful and terrifying experience of death to self, and most children of darkness would find this too difficult to undergo. The dark is more congenial to their finiteness:

> Forever falling night is a known
> Star . . .

and

> . . . the country of death is the heart's size.
>   (p. 163)

Thomas has no sooner added the final "amen" to his prayer, when he finds himself suddenly caught up in painful ecstasy. At first fearful, he would retreat to his former friends, "the dark deniers" but prayerfully accepts his purifying death in light:

I turn the corner of prayer and burn
In a blessing of the sudden
Sun. In the name of the damned
I would turn back and run
To the hidden land
But the loud sun
Christens down
The sky,
I
Am found
O let him
Scald me and drown
Me in his world's wound.
His lighting answers my
Cry. My voice burns in his hand.
Now I am lost in the blinding
One. The sun roars at the prayer's end.   (p. 165)

CONCLUSION

By his own statement, Dylan Thomas professed to be making a journey from darkness to light through the vehicle of his poetry. Critics, observing the remarkable unity of the journey, sought for a formula to describe it. Aivez used the term "process"; Daiches used the term "celebration." Following Olson's lead that Thomas was essentially a poet of the internal moral workings of the soul, we adopted the term "vision" to developing self discovery. Aware of the multitude of antithetical conflicts in Thomas' poetry, we reduced these to three major conflicts: death-life, sin-innocence, doubt-faith. These three conflicts constitute the three major problems—philosophical, moral, religious—which Thomas attempted to resolve in his journey.

We paused in chapter two to consider the poetic method of the journey and discovered that Thomas' method was essential to his intention to mirror the contradictory aspects of his experience. We examined three aspects of his poetic method: the emotional release of images, the rational control exerted over them, and the antithetical development of them. By analyzing two of his poems, we demonstrated the complexity of his poetic method by reason of a threefold activity operative in his poetry. We also proved that despite appearances to the contrary Thomas is the subject of all his poetry. This confirmed what we had proposed in chapter one about the nature of the journey.

The second part of our book was devoted to examining the journey in itself. Each of the three chapters divided itself naturally into three parts following the critical opinion that there are three distinct periods in Thomas' poetry.

Accordingly, in Chapter three, we saw Thomas journey from death to life by rejecting his morbid preoccupation with death, by growing in compassion and communion with his fellowmen, by celebrating life's fertility and resigning himself to death's inevitability.

In Chapter four, we traced Thomas' journey from sin to innocence by showing Thomas' gradual rejection of mechanical conception of man and sex, his identification of sex with sin and love with redemption, his search for pristine innocence in his lost childhood.

In Chapter five, we viewed Thomas shuffling the uncertainties and contradictions of his experience in his effort to discover reality. He was ultimately introduced to the experience of divine faith and love through his experience of human love.

Assuming the validity of our argument, there can be no doubt that Thomas did progress out of personal darkness to a light that was more than human.

BIBLIOGRAPHY

Books

(Primary Sources)

Thomas, Dylan. *The Collected Poems of Dylan Thomas*. New York: New Directions, 1953.

——. *Adventures in the Skin Trade and Other Stories*. New York: New Directions, 1964.

——. *Dylan Thomas: Letters to Vernon Watkins*. Edited by Vernon Watkins. New York: New Directions, 1957.

——. *Quite Early One Morning*. New York: New Directions, 1955.

——. *Portrait of the Artist as a Young Dog*. New Directions Paperback. New York: New Directions, 1955.

——. *Selected Writings of Dylan Thomas*. Edited by John L. L. Sweeney. New York: New Directions, 1946.

(Secondary Sources)

Bayley, J. *Romantic Survival—A Study in Poetic Evolution*. London: Constable, 1957.

Brinnin, John Malcolm (Ed.). *A Casebook on Dylan Thomas*. New York: Thomas Y. Crowell Co., 1960.

——. *Dylan Thomas in America*. Compass Book Edition. New York: The Viking Press, Inc., 1957.

Bullough, Geoffrey. *The Trend of Modern Poetry*. London: Oliver & Boyd, Ltd., 1949.

Day Lewis, Cecil. *The Poetic Image*. New York: Oxford University Press, 1948.

Deutsch, Babette. *Poetry In Our Time*. New York: Henry Holt & Company, Inc., 1952.

Drew, Elizabeth, and John L. Sweeney. *Directions in Modern Poetry*. New York: W. W. Norton & Company, Inc., 1940.

Durrell, Lawrence. *Key to Modern Poetry*. London: Peter Nevill, 1952.

Firmage, George J. (comp.) *A Garland for Dylan Thomas*. New York: Clarke & Way, Inc., 1963.

Frankenberg, Lloyd. *Pleasure Dome: On Reading Modern Poetry*. Boston: Houghton Mifflin Company, 1949.

Fraser, G. S. *Vision and Rhetoric*. New York: Barnes and Noble, 1960.

Grigson, Geoffrey. *The Harp of Aeolus and Other Essays on Art, Literature and Nature*. London: George Routledge & Sons, Ltd., 1948.

Highet, Gilbert. *Talent and Geniuses*. New York: Oxford University Press, 1957.

Holbrook, David. *Llareggub Revisited—Dylan Thomas and the State of Modern Poetry*. London: Bowes and Bowes, 1962.

Holroyd, Stuart. *Emergence from Chaos*. Boston: Houghton Mifflin Company, 1957.

Jacobi, Jolande (comp. and ed.). *Psychological Reflections—An Anthology of the Writings of C. G. Jung*. Harper Torchbook. New York: Harper & Bros., 1961.

Jennings, Elizabeth. *Christian Poetry*. "The Twentieth Century Encyclopedia of Catholicism." Vol. CXVIII. New York: Hawthorne Books, 1963.

Jones, T. H. *Dylan Thomas*. Evergreen Pilot Book. New York: Grove Press, Inc., 1963.

Korg, Jacob. *Dylan Thomas*. "Twayne's English Authors Series." New York: Twayne Publishers, Inc., 1965.

Kleinman, H. H. *The Religious Sonnets of Dylan Thomas*. "Perspectives in Criticism." Berkeley and Los Angeles: University of California Press, 1963.

Maritain, Jacques. *Creative Intuition in Art and Poetry*. First Reprint ed. New York: Meridian Books, 1955.

Maud, Ralph. *Entrances to Dylan Thomas' Poetry*. "Critical Essays in Modern Literature." Pittsburgh: University of Pittsburgh Press, 1963.

Moynihan, William T. *The Craft and Art of Dylan Thomas*. Ithaca, New York: Cornell University Press, 1966.

Olson, Elder. *The Poetry of Dylan Thomas.* Phoenix Edition. Chicago: The University of Chicago Press, 1961.

Read, Bill. *The Days of Dylan Thomas.* New York: McGraw-Hill, 1964.

Rexroth, Kenneth. *The New British Poets.* Norfolk, Conn.: New Directions, 1949.

Rolph, J. Alexander. *Dylan Thomas: A Bibliography.* New York: New Directions, 1956.

Scarfe, Francis. *Auden and After: The Liberation of Poetry, 1940-1941.* London: George Routledge & Sons, Ltd., 1942.

Stanford, Derek. *Dylan Thomas—A Literary Study.* First Paperback Edition. 1st revised ed. New York: The Citadel Press, 1964.

Tedlock, E. W. (ed.) *Dylan Thomas: The Legend and the Poet—A Collection of Biographical and Critical Essays.* London: Heinmann, 1961.

Thomas, Caitlin. *Leftover Life to Kill.* Boston: Atlantic-Little, Brown & Co., 1957.

Tindall, William York. *A Reader's Guide to Dylan Thomas.* New York: Noonday, 1962.

Treece, Henry. *Dylan Thomas: "Dog Among the Fairies."* Second Revised ed. London: Ernest Benn Ltd., 1956.

Wilder, Amos N. *Modern Poetry and the Christian Tradition.* New York: Charles Scribner's Sons, 1952.

Articles and Reviews

Adams, R. M. "Taste and Bad Taste in Metaphysical Poetry: Richard Crashaw and Dylan Thomas," *Hudson Review,* VIII (Spring, 1955), 61-77.

Aivaz, David. "The Poetry of Dylan Thomas," *Hudson Review,* III (Autumn, 1950), 382-404.

Anonymous. "The Legend of Dylan Thomas," *Time,* LXV (May 30, 1955), 90-91.

———. "A Lesson in Anatomy," *Time,* LXII (Oct. 5, 1953), 110 (A Review of *The Doctor and the Devils*).

——. "Obituary," *Poetry*, III (Jan., 1954), 244-245.

——. "Obituary," *Time*, LXII (Nov. 16, 1953), 93.

——. "Out of Tragedy a Legend and Words with Wings," *Newsweek*, L (October 28, 1957), 96.

——. "Sudden Magic," *Newsweek*, XLIV (Dec. 20, 1954), 86.

——. "Welsh Rare One," *Time*, LXI (April 6, 1953), 112 (Review of *Collected Poems*).

Barrett, Mary E. "Luncheon with Dylan Thomas," *Reporter*, X (April 27, 1954), 45-48.

Breit, Harvey. "Haunting Drama of Dylan Thomas," *The New York Times Magazine* (Oct. 6, 1957), 22ff.

Brinnin, John Malcolm. "Cockles, Brambles and Fern Hill," *Atlantic*, CXCVI (Nov., 1955), 50-55.

——. "Dylan Thomas in Wales," *Atlantic*, CXCVI (Oct., 1955), 37-44.

——. "Talent of Genius," *New Republic*, CXXX (Jan. 25, 1954), 19.

Brossard, Chandler. "The Magic of Dylan Thomas," *Commonweal*, LXII (June 10, 1955), 262-263.

Ciardi, John. "The Real Thomas," *Saturday Review*, XLI (March 1, 1958), 18f.

——. "Six Hours of Dylan Thomas," *Saturday Review*, XLI (Nov. 15, 1958), 50.

Clancy, J. P. "Dylan Thomas: Promise Clipped," *America*, XC (Dec. 12, 1953), 294-296.

Daiches, David. "The Poetry of Dylan Thomas," *College English*, XVI (1954), 50-56.

Freemantle, Anne. "Death of a Poet," *Commonweal*, LIX (Dec. 18, 1953), 285-286.

Garlick, Raymond. "The Endless Breviary," *The Month* (March, 1954), 143-145.

Garrigue, Jean. "Dark is a Way and Light is a Place," *Poetry*, XCIV (May, 1959), 111-114.

Graddon, John. "The Interior Life," *Poetry Review*, XLIV (April-June, 1953), (Review of Collected Poems), 338-340.

Gregory, Horace. *The New York Times Book Review* (July 25, 1943), 1ff. (Review of *New Poems*).

[23] Piet Smulders, *op. cit.*, p. 192.

Hamilton, E. "Words, Words, Words; The Modern School of Verse," *Saturday Review*, XXXVIII (Nov. 19, 1955), 15ff.

Hewes, Henry. "And death shall have no dominion," *Saturday Review*, XL (Oct. 19, 1957), 53.

Horan, Robert. "In Defense of Dylan Thomas," *Kenyon Review*, VII (Spring, 1945), 304-310.

Hynes, S. "Dylan Thomas: Everybody's Adonais," *Commonweal*, LIX (March 26, 1954), 628-629.

Johnson, Geoffrey. "The Acid Test," *Poetry Review*, XLIV (April-June 1953) (Review of *Collected Poems*), 340-343.

Joost, N. "Wit, Flamboyance & Faith of Dylan Thomas," *Commonweal*, LXI (Jan. 7, 1955), 387.

Kazin, Alfred. "The Posthumous Life of Dylan Thomas," *Atlantic*, CC (Oct., 1957), 164-168.

Knauber, Charles F. "Imagery of Light in Dylan Thomas," *Renascence*, VI (1954), 95-96.

Korg, J. "The Sound of Laughter," *Nation*, CLXXIX (Dec. 25, 1954), 552-553.

Lougee, David. "An Open Window," *Poetry*, XCIV (May, 1959), 114-117.

———. "Worlds of Dylan Thomas," *Poetry*, LXXXVII (Nov., 1955), 114-115.

MacNeice, Louis. "The Strange, Mighty Impact of Dylan Thomas's Poetry," *The New York Times Book Review* (April 5, 1953), 1ff. (Review of *Collected Poems*)

Maud, R. N. "Obsolete and Dialect Words as Serous Puns in Dlyan Thomas," *English Studies*, XLI (Feb., 1960), 28-30.

McDonnell, T. P. "The Emergence of Dylan Thomas," *America*, XCI (Aug. 21, 1954), 500-502.

———. "Who Killed Dylan?" *Catholic World*, CLXXXVII (July, 1958), 285-289.

Meyerhoff, H. "Violence of Dylan Thomas," *New Republic*, CXXXIII (July 11, 1955), 17-19.

Miller, J. E. Jr. "Four Cosmic Poets," *University of Kansas City Review*, XXIII (June, 1957), 312-320.

Moore, Geoffrey. "Dylan Thomas: Significance of His Genius," *Kenyon Review*, XVII (Spring, 1955), 258-277.

Moore, Nicholas. "The Poetry of Dylan Thomas," *Poetry Quarterly*, X (Winter, 1948), 229-236.

Muir, Edwin. "The Art of Dylan Thomas," *Harper's Bazaar*, LXXXVII (Feb., 1954), 128-129.

Olson, Elder. "The Poetry of Dylan Thomas," *Poetry*, LXXXIII (January, 1954), 213-220 (Review of *Collected Poems*).

Phelps, R. "In Country Dylan," *Sewanee Review*, LXII (Autumn, 1955), 681-687.

Rhys, Aneurin. "Dylan Thomas—A Further Estimate," *Poetry Review* (April-May, 1948), 214-218.

Savage, D. S. "The Poetry of Dylan Thomas," *New Republic*, CXIV (April 29, 1946), 619-622.

Scarfe, Francis. "The Poetry of Dylan Thomas," *Horizon*, II (Nov., 1940), 226-239.

Scott, Winfield Townley. "Lyric Marvel," *Saturday Review*, XXXVIII (Jan. 8, 1955), 17-18.

———. "Wild Man Bound," *Saturday Review*, XXXVI (April 11, 1953), 29-30. (Review of *Collected Poems*)

Shapiro, Karl. "Dylan Thomas," *Poetry*, LXXXVII (Nov., 1955), 100-110.

Sitwell, Edith. "Dylan Thomas," *Atlantic*, CXCIII (Feb., 1954), 42-45.

———. "The Love of Man, The Praise of God," *New York Herald Tribune Books* (May 1, 1953), 1ff. (Review of *Collected Poems*).

Spender, Stephen. "Poetry for Poetry's Sake," *Horizon*, XIII (April, 1946), 221-238.

———. Spectator, CLXXXIX (Dec. 5, 1952), 780-781.

Stearns, Marshall W. "Unsex the Skeleton: Notes on the Poetry of Dylan Thomas," *Sewanee Review*, LII (July, 1944), 424-440.

Stephens, Peter J. "Dylan Thomas: Giant Among Moderns," *New Quarterly of Poetry*, I (Winter, 1946-47), 7-11.

Sweeney, John L. "The Round Sunday Sounds," *New Republic*, CXXVIII (April 6, 1953), 24-25 (Review of *Collected Poems*).

Symons, Julian. "Obscurity and Dylan Thomas," *Kenyon Review*, II (Winter, 1940), 61-71.

Tindall, William York. "Burning and Crested Song," *American Scholar*, XXII (Autumn, 1953), 486-490. (Review of *Collected Poems*)

——. "The Poetry of Dylan Thomas," *American Scholar*, XVII (Autumn, 1948), 431-439.

Watkins, Vernon. "Behind the Fabulous Curtain," *Poetry*, XCVIII (May, 1961), 124-125.

Werry, Richard R. "The Poetry of Dylan Thomas," *College English*, XI (Feb., 1950), 250-256.

West, Anthony, "Singer and a Spectre," *The New Yorker*, XXX (Jan. 22, 1955), 106-108.

INDEX OF POEMS CITED